C000103699

THE GWENDRAETH VALLEYS RAILWAY

Kidwelly to Mynydd-y-Garreg

by
M.R.C. Price

THE OAKWOOD PRESS

© Oakwood Press & M.R.C. Price 1997

British Library Cataloguing in Publication Data
A Record for this book is available from the British Library
ISBN 0 85361 505 5

Typeset by Oakwood Graphics.
Repro by Ford Graphics, Ringwood, Hants.
Printed by The Witney Press, Witney, Oxon.

Dedication

*For Raymond, in sincere appreciation of a long friendship and much good
advice in the study of railway and industrial history.*

Title Page: The seal of the Gwendraeth Valleys Railway.

GWR Museum, Swindon/Thamesdown Borough Council

Other titles from Oakwood Press by the same author:
  Cleobury Mortimer & Ditton Priors Light Railway
  Garstang & Knott End Railway (*out of print*)
  Lambourn Valley Railway (*out of print*)
  Lampeter, Aberayron and New Quay Light Railway
  Llanelly & Mynydd Mawr Railway
  Pembroke & Tenby Railway (*out of print*)
  Saundersfoot Railway (*out of print*)
  Whitland and Cardigan Railway

In preparation:
  Burry Port & Gwendraeth Valley Railway *by Ray Bowen*

Published by
The Oakwood Press
P.O. Box 13, Usk, Mon., NP5 1YS.

Contents

A length of rusting rail in a dry stone wall by the former level crossing near Young's Brickworks, Highgate, north of Mynydd-y-Garreg. *Author*

Introduction

In its final form the Gwendraeth Valleys Railway (GVR) was a line of the utmost simplicity - little more than 2½ miles of single track running north from the South Wales main line at Kidwelly to serve the quarries of Mynydd-y-Garreg, and the tinplate works in the valley below. Away from Kidwelly there was no signalling, and 'one engine in steam' operation prevailed. There were few structures to maintain, and only a few sidings to be worked. In later years traffic was light. All this belied the line's long and intricate history. Indeed, if ever there was to be a prize for the simplest railway with the most complex history, the GVR would surely be a winner.

This book endeavours to explore that history. In doing so it has been necessary to delve not only into the story of railway promotion and politics in Carmarthenshire, but also into the story of the several industries served by the line. If there is a recurring theme it is one of brave ideas brought low, either by want of finance or by some element of dishonesty. The mineral wealth of Mynydd-y-Garreg was certainly useful, but it was never really the El Dorado that some imagined. With more careful and sustained investment it is possible that it might have done more for the local economy. Similarly, the nearby tinplate works was always undercapitalised in the 19th century, and struggling for survival. The arrival in the 20th century of some able industrialists gave the works its one period of slight success. With their departure its fortunes declined, leaving the line once again to the mineral traffic which had inspired its construction. By the 1960s it was all over, and the railway was swept away, save for the locomotive *Margaret* which remained in its shed at an amazingly intact tinplate works until 1974.

In studying the GVR I have been extremely fortunate to have the help of many local people, but most especially of Eric Hughes of Greenfield, Kidwelly. His local knowledge and enthusiasm for the history of the district was freely shared, and he was ever willing to co-operate with the all too brief appearances of a writer who lived many miles away. Much of the recent history of the GVR and local industry could not have been written without Eric's help, and I am delighted to record my appreciation.

Special mention must also be made of my friend Ray Bowen, who has again given willingly of his expertise and advice. In view of our long friendship, and his immense knowledge of the railways, canals and industry of the Gwendraeth Valley, I am especially pleased to dedicate this piece of work to him with all my thanks. Particular thanks are also due to John de Havilland, whose excellent maps do much to compensate for the dearth of good photographs of the GVR. Clearly cameras were a rarity at Mynydd-y-Garreg in years gone by, but it is hoped that the illustrations that have been found will convey something of the atmosphere of the line and the district.

Last, but by no means least, I have to thank my family for their help and patience in enabling me to complete this study. It hardly needs to be said that this book would not have been possible without them!

Martin Connop Price
Shiplake, Oxfordshire
November 1995

Chapter One

Kidwelly and its Industry Before 1850

On the east side of Carmarthen Bay, almost mid-way between the former ports of Llanelli and Carmarthen, the small town of Kidwelly stands on the banks of the Gwendraeth Fach. This energetic river flows into the town from the north, passing the little villages of Llangendeirne and Llandyfaelog in a valley of green and pleasant pastures. The name 'Gwendraeth' means 'white strand' or 'white beach', and the Gwendraeth Fach meets the Gwendraeth Fawr in a vast expanse of sand, mud and marsh south and west of Kidwelly. The Gwendraeth Fawr River approaches from the east down a wider valley, having passed the coal mining villages of Pontyberem, Ponthenry and Pontyates. Indeed, apart from the small Pembrokeshire coalfield, the Gwendraeth Fawr valley represents the western extremity of the South Wales coalfield, and even in the 1990s sizeable tonnages of high grade anthracite are being extracted from open-cast mines. Between the two valleys stands a prominent limestone ridge, known at its southern end as Mynydd-y-Garreg - 'the mountain of rock'. On a clear day it is easy to see the monastic island of Caldey, off Tenby, and the coast of North Devon, as well as the nearby town of Kidwelly.

Once a trading port in its own right, Kidwelly's most prominent feature has long been the magnificent Norman castle which dominates the skyline. Built between 1106 and 1116 by Roger, Bishop of Salisbury, the castle was a typical Norman motte and bailey design and was intended to enable Roger to secure his grip on lands ceded to him by King Henry I. Numerous skirmishes took place in the early years, the most notable of which occurred in 1136. On that occasion the castle was attacked by the forces of Gwenllian, the wife of a Welsh prince. She was defeated and taken prisoner, but the engagement is still recalled in the name of a farm, Maesgwenllian, situated about one mile north of the castle.

The history of the castle and the town of Kidwelly are in many ways intertwined. In 1274 the castle was rebuilt, making much more extensive use of stone, and in 1280 the town itself was walled. In 1315 the castle was rebuilt again, the addition of residential accommodation, a chapel and enhanced defences giving the structure the layout still visible today. No doubt these improvements gave local people an added sense of security, because the same 14th century witnessed a period of considerable growth for Kidwelly as a commercial centre. Indeed, it is said that at this time the several small quays on the tidal reaches of the Gwendraeth Fach made Kidwelly the busiest trading port in South Wales. By the later part of the 16th century all this had changed. The river was subject to silting, deterring the larger sailing vessels. Furthermore, after many years of relative peace the castle was virtually deserted, the officers in particular favouring more comfortable homes in the town and adjoining countryside. By 1615 parts of the building were in ruins, and local people were stripping it of lead and timber for their own use. Eventually the castle passed into the hands of the Earl of Cawdor, but even in the period of the Civil War it never really regained military significance.

The other prominent feature of the Kidwelly skyline is the spire of St Mary's Parish Church. The building dates from the 12th century, and its spacious interior reflects the prosperity of the town in the medieval era. The priory, which once lay to the north of the church, came to an end with the dissolution of the monasteries in the time of Henry VIII, and nothing now remains. In its time the church has been visited by all the notable figures in the history of the town, and at least two figures prominent in its industrial history are interred there. These are Charles Gwynn, founder of the Kidwelly Tinplate Works and Thomas Kymer, builder of the first canal in Wales, Kymer's Canal in the valley of the Gwendraeth Fawr. However they were not the very first people to show an interest in the industrial potential of the district.

According to W.J. Lewis in his authoritative work *Lead Mining in Wales* (Cardiff, 1967) there were said to be mines of coal, lead and iron in the Lordship of Kidwelly as early as 1581. Over 130 years later, in 1717, Dr John Lane of Bristol, then described as a 'mining adventurer' was granted a lease by Kidwelly Corporation to search for copper and other minerals on the ridge behind the town known as Mynydd-y-Garreg. A clause in the lease gave Lane the right to set up 'mills or engines', and by 1721 he had established a stamping mill to crush ore at a crossing point on the Gwendraeth Fach river known as Bank Broadford. It is thought that this development probably included the building of a dam across the river, and the provision of a leat to serve a waterwheel at the stamping mill. Unfortunately it was all short-lived, because in 1726 Lane went bankrupt, and by 1735 his mill was said to be in ruins.

Charles Gwynn of Kidwelly, described simply as a 'tinman', was given licence in August 1737 to build rolling and tin mills on the site of Lane's unsuccessful enterprise at Bank Broadford. Accordingly the Kidwelly Tin Works came into being, and in October 1737 Gwynn was granted authority to quarry stone on Mynydd-y-Garreg for building purposes. In the following year Gwynn formed a partnership with Anthony Rogers of Carmarthen, who provided additional financial backing. Before long Rogers' finance made him the dominant partner, so that by the time the partnership ended in 1747 he was able to buy out Gwynn for just £70. Thereafter Rogers obtained a new lease of the tinworks in his own name, whilst Gwynn became involved in business in Llanelli, and in searching for minerals around Mynydd-y-Garreg.

Anthony Rogers died in 1756, and he was succeeded by his son, Lewis Rogers. In 1758 Lewis formed a partnership with the notable Carmarthen ironfounder, Robert Morgan, presumably hoping to benefit from Morgan's experience and financial resources. It did not prove to be a particularly happy relationship, with numerous arguments over the state of the Kidwelly works and over money. The partnership was terminated by Lewis Rogers in 1761, prompting Morgan to set up his own tinplate works adjacent to his iron furnaces in Carmarthen. In the following year Rogers found himself a new partner in the person of Thomas Price of Glamorgan, who also had considerable experience of the iron trade. Although Price was never very prominent, the new arrangement appears to have been more successful, with the Kidwelly works finding some growth in the ensuing years.

Lewis Rogers was active in public life in Kidwelly for some years, and was

Mayor twice (1763 and 1767). He was also a Commissioner appointed under an Act of Parliament of 1766 which authorised the construction of Thomas Kymer's canal between Kidwelly and Pwllyllygod, to serve collieries near Carway in the Gwendraeth Fawr valley. When this opened in 1769 it was the earliest commercial canal in the Principality. When Rogers died in 1776 his sister and her husband, Leonard Bilson Gwynn, became the administrators of his estate, and as such they obtained a new lease of the tinworks in 1777. Unfortunately Rogers' will was contested by his numerous creditors, who brought a law suit against Gwynn. Eventually the Court of Chancery ordered the sale of the estate in the late 1780s, and it was purchased by Gwynn for the sum of £1,370. As the works had already been sub-let to Messrs Morris and Roderick, their partnership was allowed to continue until they themselves ended the arrangement in, or by, 1792.

The works were left idle for some years, and after Gwynn's death in 1798 it fell to his widow, Catherine, to respond to a notice from the Kidwelly Corporation requiring the repair of the tin mills. The outcome was the sale of the works in 1801 to Messrs Haselwood, Hathaway and Perkins, who soon set about the reconstruction of the premises. Haselwood, the managing partner appears to have been better as a manufacturer than as a businessman, because after his death in 1806 it emerged that the works was in serious financial difficulties. Perkins dissolved his partnership with Hathaway in 1807, and by 1808 the business was in the hands of a Carmarthen banker and former trustee of the works named Thomas Waters. No doubt assisted by the demands of the Napoleonic wars, production increased, and in 1815 Kidwelly was close to matching the output of Carmarthen. Waters died when relatively young in 1816, and a new lease of the premises was granted to his friend Philip Protheroe. In turn, he sub-let to a noted ironfounder, Philip Vaughan, who manufactured tinplate on the site until 1829.

During Thomas Waters' time at the tin works a number of local landowners recognised a need to develop transport facilities in the district. On 15th September, 1810, the *Carmarthen Journal* carried a notice of a meeting to be held two days later at the Pelican Inn, Kidwelly, 'for persons interested in the improvement of the Port and Harbour of Kidwelly, and of the Land and Coal Owners in the surrounding district . . .' The same issue carried a separate notice stating that 'application is intended to be made to Parliament in the ensuing Session for obtaining an Act for restoring, improving and maintaining the navigation of the Gwendraeth Fach and Gwendraeth Fawr, for the making and maintaining of a Dock, Basin and Reservoir or Floating Harbour . . . and also for making and maintaining navigable cuts or canals and tramroads or railways . . . to communicate with the said Port and Harbour'. In brief, the limitations of Kidwelly as a port were acknowledged, and the district was making a determined attempt to improve its own prospects.

In fact it took another year of debate before the landowners, led in 1811 by Lord Cawdor, were ready to present a Bill to Parliament. In 1812 this was approved, and the preamble to the Act provided for the construction of the Kidwelly & Llanelly Canal - essentially canal extensions from Kymer's Canal at Spudder's Bridge, in the Gwendraeth Fawr Valley, with a few associated tramroads. According to the Act, the canal company were empowered to build tramroad branches 'to and from a certain Limestone Quarry at a certain place called Mynydd-y-Garreg to the said Kymers Canal at or near a certain place there called Pont Morris Cross [Tycoch] and also another branch to or from . . . Kidwelly Tin Mills to the said Kidwelly Canal at or near . . . Pont Morris Cross'. In the event the Kidwelly & Llanelly Canal Co. concentrated its efforts on building its principal portions of canal towards Llanelly and up the Gwendraeth, and these feeder tramroads were never built. However they can be recorded as the earliest tramway scheme intended to serve both Kidwelly and Mynydd-y-Garreg.

A new era began at Kidwelly when the tenancy of the works was granted to a civil engineer named Thomas Hay. His father had worked for the Earl of Ashburnham on his collieries and canal and feeder tramroads near Pembrey, and although the technology was quite basic, the father's experience of management may have given the son some useful insights. At all events, under his leadership the tinworks did well, and records survive of exports to many parts of the country. Unfortunately, as was so often the case at Kidwelly, the management changed after only a few years, in this case before Hay had managed to make much progress towards adding ironworks facilities to the available plant.

In 1838 the tenancy passed to H.H. Downman, who continued to invest in more iron working equipment, but at the expense of cluttering the restricted tinworks site. The company became known as the Kidwelly Iron & Tinplate Co., and by 1839 pig iron was being imported from the famous Neath Abbey Ironworks to be converted into bars. The rather inexperienced Downman was not a talented businessman, because in 1841 he was declared bankrupt. For a time care of the works was transferred to his brother, but even when in partnership they did not prosper. Indeed, they seem to have been much occupied with the business of raising loans, and then struggling with the consequences when the repayments could not be made. Between 1846 and 1848 the Downmans lost control, but despite his earlier failure H.H. Downman managed to purchase the tinworks again in 1848. Unfortunately the old pattern repeated itself, and within a few years Downman was in difficulty with his creditors, one of whom was Crawshay Bailey, son of the famous iron master. Early in 1858 Downman died, and Bailey had the works put up for sale. After such a chequered history perhaps it was not surprising that it took two years to find a buyer!

If the story of the tinplate works became a story of many disappointments, the story of Kidwelly itself had one new and very positive feature in the 1840s - the coming of the railway. Surveyed in 1844 by the celebrated engineer Isambard Kingdom Brunel, the South Wales Railway was intended to run from a junction with the Great Western Railway near Gloucester by way of Chepstow, Newport, Cardiff, Bridgend, Neath and Swansea. In its initial form this broad gauge (7 ft 0¼ in.) railway was proposed to run over an inland route from Llanelli to Carmarthen across the Gwendraeth valley, but in the event it was decided to adopt a cheaper alignment by following first the coastline to Kidwelly and Ferryside, and then the Towy estuary up to Carmarthen. Work on this section began in 1847, but delays arose as the Directors of the South Wales Railway felt obliged by the fact of famine in Ireland to reconsider the site of the western terminus of the line, intended as a packet port for Irish traffic. After much deliberation it was decided to take the line to Neyland on Milford Haven rather than to Fishguard, on Pembrokeshire's north coast.

In its original form the railway from Swansea to Carmarthen comprised a broad gauge single track of Barlow rails, crossing the Gwendraeth Fach at Kidwelly by a timber bridge with wrought iron lifting sections. As such it was opened on 11th October, 1852, and an extension to Haverfordwest was made ready for use by the end of 1853. The opening of the South Wales Railway appears to have helped to open minds to new commercial ideas, because in Carmarthenshire the 1850s soon became a decade of new economic endeavour. Not only were other railways proposed, most notably the Carmarthen & Cardigan Railway, but new activities were attempted - for example silica brick making at Kidwelly. The time was ripe for further development.

The kilns on the hillside in the distance are thought to be those built by Owen Bowen *c.* 1863. The larger kilns in the foreground were built by Edward Threlfall in 1872.

Roger Worsley

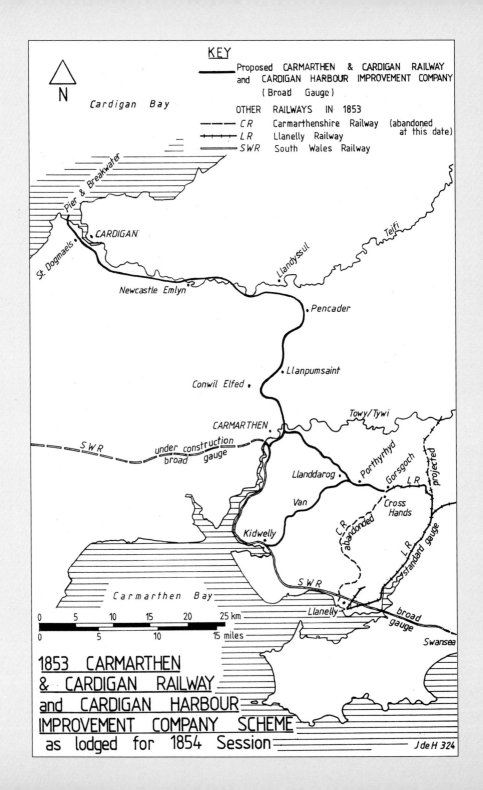

KEY

Proposed CARMARTHEN & CARDIGAN RAILWAY
and CARDIGAN HARBOUR IMPROVEMENT COMPANY
(Broad Gauge)

OTHER RAILWAYS IN 1853

CR Carmarthenshire Railway (abandoned
at this date)
LR Llanelly Railway
SWR South Wales Railway

N

Cardigan Bay

Pier & Breakwater

St. Dogmaels

CARDIGAN

Teifi

Llandyssul

Newcastle Emlyn

Pencader

Llanpumsaint

Conwil Elfed

Towy/Tywi

CARMARTHEN

SWR   under construction
broad   gauge

Llanddarog

Porthyrhyd

Gorsgoch

LR

projected

Van

CR
abandoned

Cross
Hands

Kidwelly

LR

standard gauge

SWR

Carmarthen Bay

Llanelly

broad
gauge

Swansea

0   5   10   15   20   25 km

0   5   10   15 miles

1853 CARMARTHEN
& CARDIGAN RAILWAY
and CARDIGAN HARBOUR
IMPROVEMENT COMPANY SCHEME
as lodged for 1854 Session

J de H 324

Chapter Two

The Carmarthen & Cardigan Era

The original and main intention of the promoters of the Carmarthen & Cardigan Railway (C&CR) was to construct a link between the South Wales Railway at Carmarthen and the town of Cardigan, situated some 35 miles away, near the mouth of the River Teifi. By 1853, though, they had several other ambitious ideas. One was to seek powers to extend the line about five miles west of Cardigan to a new deep water harbour to be built on the coast beyond St Dogmaels, this work to be carried out in conjunction with another new undertaking, the Cardigan Harbour Improvement Company. The other proposals were for some 23 miles of railways intended primarily for mineral traffic.

The main mineral branch was to be built east-south-east from Carmarthen by way of Llanddarog to a point about one mile east of Porthyrhyd, near a public house known as Mansell's Arms. The engineering of this section promised to be heavy, and the gradients alarming. At Mansell's Arms there was to be a junction, with one branch turning away to the south along a limestone ridge towards Van and Kidwelly on the South Wales Railway. The other line continued eastwards towards the anthracite collieries on Mynydd Mawr near Cross Hands. At this period the early Carmarthenshire Railway or Tramroad was out of use in the vicinity of Cross Hands, and it was proposed that the mineral branch should terminate nearby at Gorsgoch, where it would meet the Mountain branch of the standard gauge Llanelly Railway.

In November 1853, it was estimated that all these railways could be built for £882,000, whilst the Cardigan Harbour improvements would cost the rather convenient sum of £118,000. Accordingly the Directors decided to go to Parliament for powers to carry out these works and permission to raise capital of £1 million in £10 shares. Figures of this magnitude must have seemed immensely impressive in rural Wales, and the minutes of Kidwelly Corporation noted a few weeks earlier that

> ... the Mayor and Aldermen ... having been informed that the Carmarthen & Cardigan Railway Company intend to have a branch line extending from the Gorslas and Cross Hands district of collieries and passing near Crwbin and Capel Dydden Limekilns to Van and from thence to the station of the South Wales Railway at Kidwelly ... resolved that this Corporation do give the said railway company all the co-operation, support and assistance ... in their power.

Unfortunately the glowing forecasts for the company erred heavily on the side of optimism, and the initial appeal for subscribers to the scheme did not match the hopes of the promoters. As early as Christmas 1853, it was obvious that the necessary funds would not be found. In addition, the South Wales Railway (SWR) was not at all happy about the suggested branch railway between Porthyrhyd and Kidwelly, possibly perceiving that it might be used as an alternative through route to Carmarthen. The outcome was a decision to prune back the proposals in order to nurture a more realistic scheme. After a good deal of heart searching the Directors accepted their solicitor's advice and reduced their application to Parliament to a plan to build 25½ miles of railway from the SWR at Carmarthen to the small town of Newcastle Emlyn. In this form the C&CR obtained its Act in 1854, and to enable it to fulfil the project powers were granted to raise £300,000 in £10 shares, and a further £80,000 by borrowing.

One of the company's main promoters was a certain Edward Fitzwilliams, who had hoped to see the railway serve his limestone workings near Van. Disappointed by the change of plan, Fitzwilliams retired from the Board, and later left the country. During the 1850s the idea of constructing a railway to serve the limestone quarries near Van and Kidwelly had to take second place to the company's primary aim, but even this was not easily achieved. As authorised the line was to be built to the 7 ft gauge, the broad gauge favoured by Isambard Kingdom Brunel, the Engineer to both the Great Western Railway and the South Wales Railway. In 1856 a contract to construct the section to Llandyssil was granted to Messrs Jay of London, the C&CR's Engineer being Joseph Cubitt. Costs soon began to mount, and in 1859 the company went back to Parliament for permission to construct the line to the standard gauge of 4 ft 8½ in. The South Wales Railway was incensed by this proposal, but eventually persuaded the C&CR to withdraw its Bill by undertaking to work the new line as far as Carmarthen Tin Works at its own expense. This first mile was ready for traffic by 1st November, 1859, but was not opened with official Board of Trade consent until 1st March, 1860.

Construction continued, and six more miles to Conwil were opened on 3rd September, 1860. Before very long, though, the high cost of hiring locomotives and rolling stock from the South Wales Railway became too much to bear, and the working arrangement was terminated at the end of December 1860. To add insult to injury, the SWR proceeded to remove rails valued at £1,343 to compensate itself for losses arising from working the line. As the Carmarthen & Cardigan Railway had relied entirely upon the South Wales Railway for rolling stock and motive power, all traffic ceased. The Directors were faced with an urgent need to acquire their own engines, and in due course two locomotives were hired from Sharp, Stewart & Co., and stock obtained from the Oldbury Carriage Co. On this basis they were able to re-open the line from Carmarthen Junction to Conwil on 12th August, 1861.

After this unhappy and expensive episode a period of restraint and consolidation might have been deemed appropriate. Although the company was already in financial difficulties, the Directors decided to revive several of their early ideas. As the powers to extend the line beyond Llandyssil to Newcastle Emlyn had lapsed, the top priority was to get this authority renewed. In addition, however, they sought powers to build three quite separate railways in the vicinity of Kidwelly. One was for a branch from the South Wales Railway to a point close to the limestone outcrop at Mynydd-y-Garreg. Another was for a branch from Kidwelly to Carway colliery in the Gwendraeth Fawr valley, closely following much of the route of Kymer's Canal of 1769. The third was for an extension of the line from Carway up the hillside to the former

Carmarthenshire Railway at Cwm Blawd, near Pontyberem, gaining access to the old trackbed leading to the collieries of Mynydd Mawr. On the assumption that the C&CR could negotiate running powers over the SWR between Kidwelly and Carmarthen Junction, all these proposals were intended to generate regular and increased freight traffic, especially in lime and coal. At this period lime was a basic requirement for agricultural development wherever the soil was at all acidic, and there was considerable potential for lime traffic extending far beyond the naturally acidic soils of Carmarthenshire and Cardiganshire. Similarly it was believed that coal would be required not only for domestic and industrial purposes, but also for lime-burning.

The logic behind these proposals was plain enough, and almost certainly the greatest enthusiast for these extensions was the company Secretary, Owen Bowen. Appointed as early as November 1853, Bowen was never just another company servant. The minutes of the C&CR show that he undertook a wide range of tasks on behalf of the Board, and that he enjoyed considerable powers of management. Already a landowner and a man of means, he was instrumental in the formation of the Carway & Duffryn Steam Coal Co. Ltd, and when this company was registered on 1st January, 1858, he was again company Secretary rather than a Director. Plainly his involvement in this company was a powerful reason for him to look forward to the building of a railway up the valley of the Gwendraeth Fawr.

According to minutes of the Kidwelly Corporation dated 21st October, 1861, an application was made on behalf of Mr Owen Bowen for the consent of the Corporation 'to his making a mineral line from Mynydd-y-Garreg over part of their property, and also to ask them to sell him the reversion of the leasehold and the fee simple of the freehold, and also to have to work any limestone adjoining his lease on payment of 2d./ton royalty'. The Corporation consented to these requests 'provided that the line be made in two years from this time at a fair valuation . . .' The stipulation about time was soon shown to be unrealistic, because the C&CR's plans encountered opposition from the prominent local landowner, Lord Dynevor. In February 1862, the Corporation resolved unanimously to petition the House of Commons 'asking them to suspend their standing orders in favour of Mynydd-y-Garreg and Kidwelly and other branches of the Carmarthen & Cardigan Railway'. This was naive and wishful thinking, and on this occasion the necessary legislation was lost.

In spite of this setback the Corporation agreed, in August 1862, to give Owen Bowen a 99-year lease to raise and work stone on part of Mynydd-y-Garreg. Six months later, with the appropriate legislation again before Parliament, the Corporation resolved to sell 'the reversion of all land Mr Bowen may require on the route of the railway, belonging to them, Mr Bowen to pay full compensation to the leaseholders'.

The Corporation minutes are notable for the frequency of their references to Owen Bowen, and their only occasional mention of the Carmarthen & Cardigan Railway, leaving the reader with the conviction that initiative for the venture must have come from Bowen himself. His lease of limestone at Mynydd-y-Garreg appears to have been personal, and according to the Revd D. Daven Jones, a group of limekilns at Mynydd-y-Garreg was the work of 'Owen Bowen of London'. That he had a business address in London appears to be some measure of his prosperity, and 4 Chatham Place, Blackfriars, was the venue for many C&CR Board meetings. Indeed, it seems likely that Bowen had a key role in keeping English investors in touch with events in West Wales. In 1863 he leased a property on Pinged Hill, Kidwelly, and in the following year he presented the town of Kidwelly with a clock which was installed in the spire of St Mary's Church. He was described then 'as a pioneer of the Mynydd-y-Garreg railway and lime works'. Even so, it was not until April 1864 that the Corporation decided that Bowen should pay £900 for the land it had agreed to sell him two years earlier, and upon which some clearance and construction may have taken place already.

Although Owen Bowen appears to have been successful financially, the Carmarthen & Cardigan Railway was not. Quite apart from the objections of Lord Dynevor, it was not at all clear in 1862 that it had the means to pursue all its stated aims. Accordingly Parliament renewed the company's authority to build between Llandyssil and Newcastle Emlyn, but would not consent to the branches. The Directors (doubtless encouraged by Bowen) could not accept this as a conclusion. A year later they had another Bill before Parliament seeking branches at Kidwelly and an extension of the main line from Newcastle Emlyn to Cardigan. Again the branches had to be abandoned, although approval was given for the extension to Cardigan. Eventually, in 1864, the Carmarthen & Cardigan Railway obtained an Act enabling the company to build a 6½ mile branch from Kidwelly by way of Mynydd-y-Garreg and Van to a point north of Velindre known as Limestone Hill. The latter name indicated the whole object of the exercise, and indeed for company purposes this branch became known simply as 'the lime line'. The other intended branch running further east into the Gwendraeth Valley to Carway, and on to Pontyberem, became known as 'the coal line'; in 1865 the company eventually succeeded in obtaining its Act to build this branch also. However to state these facts so briefly is to gloss over a great deal of activity in the intervening years. The C&CR Acts of 1864 and 1865 provided the legal foundations upon which the Gwendraeth Valleys Railway was constructed, but to understand these developments fully it is necessary to consider the background in greater detail.

Chapter Three

Crisis on the C&CR, 1862-1865

The minutes of the Carmarthen & Cardigan Board between 1862 and 1865 reveal much of the thinking of both the Directors and the company Secretary, Owen Bowen. Initially Bowen seems to have been especially concerned for the proposed 'coal line', no doubt thinking that anything that would help his coal to move from Carway to the customer, preferably in the same wagons, was worthy of his energy and attention. At a Board meeting held on 27th October, 1862, Mr Coates, the company's solicitor, recommended one Parliamentary Bill for all the mineral branches. Bowen objected on the grounds that opponents to one part of the Bill might oppose it in its entirety, even if not actually hostile to other parts of it. The solicitor replied that if necessary the C&CR could give up the line from Carway to Pontyberem, or the coal lines altogether, and try for the rest. In response Bowen demonstrated his concern for the lime line also, observing that 'as by the lime line as now laid out coal could be brought down by canal and put into broad gauge trucks at Kidwelly'. When it was pointed out that the C&CR faced opposition from the Kidwelly & Llanelly Canal Co., Bowen suggested that this could be overcome if powers were taken out to purchase the canal and harbour works from that company as an alternative scheme to making the mineral railways. The solicitor declared that this would involve additional work and expense. Accordingly it was resolved that the company should promote two Parliamentary Bills, one for the extension of the main line from Newcastle Emlyn to Cardigan, and the other for the mineral branches from Kidwelly. In passing Mr Coates mentioned that it would be desirable for a company independent of the C&CR to be formed for the purpose of making the lime line, but the Directors did not pursue the point. Even so, this was the first hint that the C&CR and the lime line might have to be separate.

In 1863, as already mentioned, Parliament approved an extension of the C&CR between Llandyssil and Newcastle Emlyn, but the proposals for branches from Kidwelly did not proceed, not least because the 'coal line' to Carway and Pontyberem was viewed unfavourably by both Lord Dynevor's agent and the Kidwelly & Llanelly Canal Co. As a result Owen Bowen's anxiety over the way the plans were presented to Parliament proved to be justified, but even before the fate of this Bill had been determined he was pressing on with his plans on the assumption that in due course they would be successful. In April 1863, he told the Board that he had been negotiating with the Dynevor estate for a piece of land required for the railway at Mynydd-y-Garreg; he had also applied to another landowner Mr Colby, for a portion of land at Kidwelly.

On 12th May, 1863, Owen Bowen reported a meeting he had had with the Secretary and the solicitor of the Kidwelly & Llanelly Canal Co., at which he had suggested using the canal bank between Tycoch bridge, and the railway bridge at Kidwelly 'for the purpose of running a siding from the South Wales Railway at Kidwelly down to the canal, and so loading coals from barges and broad gauge trucks'. Evidently the interview ended with Bowen proposing that

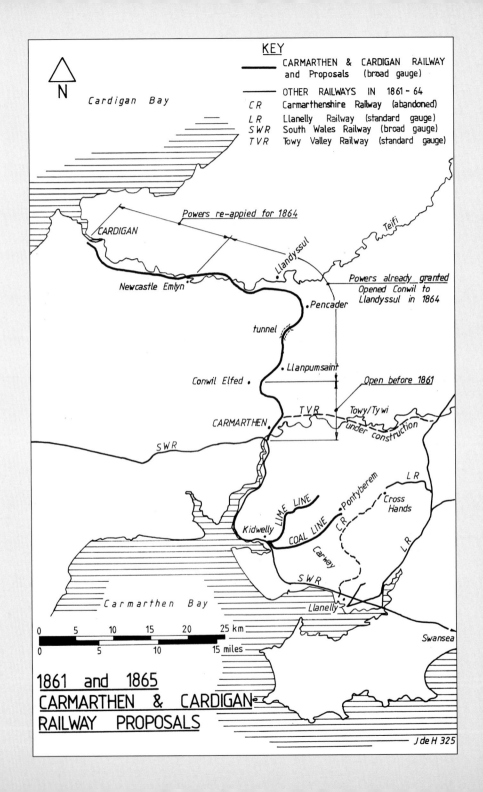

KEY

CARMARTHEN & CARDIGAN RAILWAY
and Proposals (broad gauge)

OTHER RAILWAYS IN 1861 – 64

CR Carmarthenshire Railway (abandoned)
LR Llanelly Railway (standard gauge)
SWR South Wales Railway (broad gauge)
TVR Towy Valley Railway (standard gauge)

Cardigan Bay

N

Teifi

Powers re-applied for 1864

CARDIGAN

Llandyssul

Newcastle Emlyn

Powers already granted
Opened Conwil to
Llandyssul in 1864

Pencader

tunnel

Llanpumsaint

Open before 1861

Conwil Elfed

TVR   *Towy/Tywi*

CARMARTHEN   under construction

SWR

LR

Pontyberem   Cross
Hands

CR

LIME LINE

Kidwelly

COAL LINE

Carway

SWR

LR

Carmarthen Bay

Llanelly

0   5   10   15   20   25 km
0   5   10   15 miles

Swansea

1861 and 1865
CARMARTHEN & CARDIGAN
RAILWAY PROPOSALS

J de H 325

if the canal company 'would procure the assent of Lord Dynevor to this company (C&CR) renewing this session their application for making a line to Mynydd-y-Garreg, and if this company were successful in getting the Act . . ., (they) would enter into an agreement with the canal company not to promote, or aid in promoting, a railway up the Gwendraeth Valley to Carway and Pontyberem'.

The C&CR Directors endorsed this pledge provided the assent of Lord Dynevor was obtained. However, in the event of the company failing to get an Act of Parliament in that session it would not be prejudiced by the arrangement, or prohibited from renewing its application for the mineral branches in the next session. The Chairman of the C&CR, John L. Propert, accompanied by John Wright of the engineers, Messrs Cubitt & Wright, actually travelled to Paris to meet Lord Dynevor. What this excursion did for the Carmarthen & Cardigan's expense account is not recorded, but it proved to be a complete waste of time, Lord Dynevor being unwilling to consent to anything without the agreement of Mr Bishop, his agent.

The weeks went by without significant progress, and all opportunity of obtaining Parliamentary approval for the Kidwelly branches in 1863 was lost. Accordingly that autumn the Directors decided to concentrate their efforts on obtaining powers in 1864 to build the 'lime line' from Kidwelly to Mynydd-y-Garreg, Van, and Limestone Hill. By 1st March, 1864, no petition had been lodged against the Bill, and the Board noted certain observations made by Lord Redesdale on the financing of the line. As a result the Board resolved 'that the capital of the Kidwelly branch railway do form a separate capital, and that after reserving to the subscribers 5 per cent of the net profits arising therefrom, the surplus form part of the profits of the general undertaking . . .' This appears to have been the first formal move towards making the new line quite distinct from the C&CR.

The Bill received the Royal Assent on 28th April, 1864. Clause 3 described the line of the railway. Having made a Junction at Kidwelly with the South Wales Railway (actually then recently taken over by the Great Western Railway), the line was to 'pass through the Parish of Kidwelly, Llangendeirne, Llechdwnny, Gwempa, and Velindre, and shall terminate in or near a field in the Hamlet of Velindre, belonging to Rawleigh Adenbrook Mansell Esquire, . . . and the said Railway shall be constructed upon the Broad Gauge of seven feet, or upon a Mixed Gauge'. The Act specified that the railway should be completed within three years, on pain of a financial penalty. The C&CR was authorised to raise up to £100,000 in Carmarthen & Cardigan (Kidwelly Branch) shares, which capital was to be kept quite distinct from that of the main undertaking. The company was also given powers to borrow up to £33,300 on mortgage.

When the C&CR Directors met on 1st July, 1864, they recognised the provisions of the Act by resolving not only that the Kidwelly branch shares should form a separate capital, but also that they 'should be entitled to a yearly dividend out of profits arising from the Kidwelly branch railway at the rate of 6 per cent to the total exclusion of participation in profits of the rest of the company's undertaking.' It was also agreed that any surplus profit arising from the Kidwelly branch applicable to dividends above 6 per cent per annum

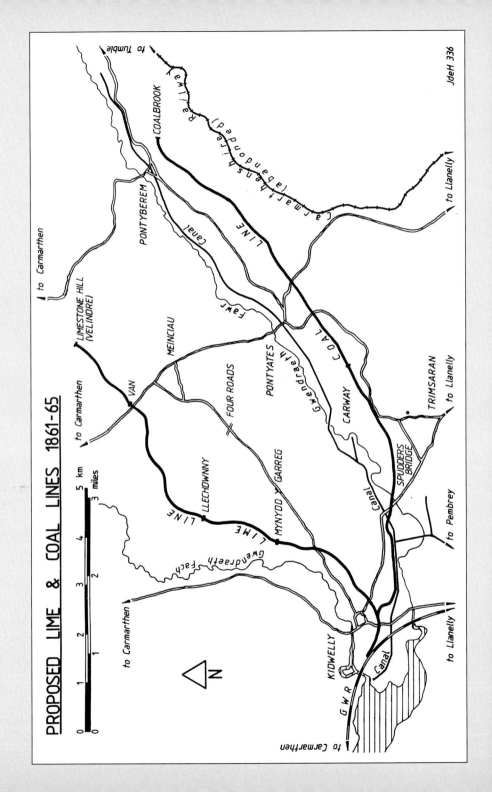

PROPOSED LIME & COAL LINES 1861-65

JdeH 336

to Tumble

COALBROOK

Carmarthenshire Railway (abandoned)

to Llanelly

to Carmarthen

PONTYBEREM

Canal

LINE

LIMESTONE HILL (VELINDRE)

Fawr

MEINCIAU

VAN

to Carmarthen

FOUR ROADS

PONTYATES

COAL

Gwendraeth

CARWAY

TRIMSARAN

to Llanelly

5 km

miles

LINE

LLECHDWNNY

LIME

MYNYDD Y GARREG

Gwendraeth Fach

Canal

SPUDDERS BRIDGE

to Pembrey

to Carmarthen

N

KIDWELLY

G W R

Canal

to Llanelly

to Carmarthen

should be assigned to the general shareholders of the company. With all the advantages of hindsight, such optimism seems quite touching.

Whilst the lawyers and Parliament had been considering the finer details of the legislation, the company had pressed on with further land acquisition. In June the Directors agreed to appoint Mr Cubitt as their consulting engineer on a retainer of £50 per annum, whilst Mr Wright was appointed Engineer to the company for the construction of the line from Llandyssil to Newcastle Emlyn, and for the mineral branches from Kidwelly. For the former he was to be paid during construction at the rate of £500 per annum, and for the latter the very impressive sum of £1,000 per annum. The minutes offer no clues as to how the Directors supposed such sums could be sustained.

The contractor was to be Howard Ashton Holden, and later details emerged of the somewhat curious basis for his appointment. As early as 1861 an agreement had been made whereby,

> Mr Holden shall have the privilege, and the company shall give him the option of undertaking the construction of all such extensions or branches of the railway as the company may hereafter be empowered to construct upon the like terms and conditions referred to (in the accompanying specification) and at like prices to be satisfied by the Bonds of the company.

At this period it was common for contractors to be paid partly in the shares or bonds of the company employing them, and as the share capital of the C&CR was far from fully subscribed, the company specialised in issuing Lloyds' bonds to cover its expenditure. The recipient of such a bond had a document which stated the sum owed and the future date at which it would be repaid with interest. On the strength of this a contractor could obtain a loan, although the bond would usually be taken at a discount. In the early 1860s Lloyds' bonds were widely used and accepted, but much of this paper was of very doubtful value. At the time the C&CR bonds must have looked like reasonable security; the unfortunate reality was that they were being issued recklessly, by a company that had very little to back them up.

At all events, in 1861, before a Bill had been presented to Parliament, Mr Holden elected to take the contract for the Kidwelly branch on the same terms as then applied for the construction of the C&CR to Llandyssil. Furthermore, it seems that in August 1861 he applied to the Board for bonds to the value of £20,000 'on account of his contract for the Kidwelly works'. The company Secretary, Owen Bowen, advised the Directors that the works executed by the contractor did not warrant the issue of this amount of bonds, 'but taking into account that Mr Holden would have to provide several thousand pounds for land for the Spudders Bridge line (i.e. the coal line), and that that amount of money would be required before the next Board meeting, it was under all the circumstances not unreasonable on the part of Mr Holden to make the application'. The Board duly resolved to issue bonds worth £20,000.

Who was kidding who? At this moment in 1861 the C&CR had no powers to build the branches at Kidwelly, nor any very immediate prospect of possessing them. Furthermore the company was already effectively insolvent, being in debt to the original contractor for the Llandyssil line, a Mr Jay of London. The only urgency was to find fresh funds, and as this should have been obvious to everyone in the company, it is tempting to suppose that at least some of those involved had some hidden agenda. Owen Bowen's activities were so central to all the company's concerns at Kidwelly, it may be assumed that he was instrumental in setting up the arrangement with Holden, and in persuading the Board to accept it. Although positive proof is lacking, it seems entirely likely that Bowen was using his position with the C&CR to advance his own industrial interests, regardless of the long-term implications of his actions for the railway. Furthermore, he may have favoured Holden simply because of the contractor's willingness to accept Lloyds' bonds. To judge from a C&CR personal accounts ledger for this period, Holden not only received payments for construction work and materials, but also for ordinary maintenance of the railway's permanent way. The most startling figures, though, come under the heading 'discount commission'. Whilst the term is not defined, and may never be fully understood, it would seem that by 1865 Holden had received the enormous sum of £117,942 under this heading, implying an immense amount of dealing in bonds and loans.

At all events, Holden became the contractor for the Llandyssil line as well as the Kidwelly branches, and (no doubt to the relief of all concerned) in June 1864 he managed to complete the railway to Llandyssil. At the same period he was paid sizeable sums in Lloyds' bonds in respect of the Kidwelly branches. In July 1864, for example, he requested and received bonds with a face value of £15,000. In so far as Holden was directly involved in land purchase there was some justification for a payment, but it is not at all clear whether the company was getting value for money. In the same month Owen Bowen was also engaged in land acquisition, by trying to buy land to enable the proposed coal line to be extended to a point in the Gwendraeth Valley north of Spudders' Bridge. He endeavoured to justify this premature step by saying that if such land could be secured 'it would add greatly to the value of this company's line at Kidwelly, and facilitate Parliamentary powers being obtained in the next session of Parliament for making the coal line branch'.

That autumn a Bill for the coal line was promoted in Parliament, but the C&CR's finances were in such a parlous state it must be doubtful whether the company actually paid for it, or whether it was funded by those most likely to benefit, for example, Owen Bowen. Indeed, the company's cavalier attitude to money was now catching up with it, and in November 1864 a Receiver was appointed by the Court of Chancery. The ensuing enquiry into the company's finances painted a picture of utter chaos. The liabilities were in excess of £1 million, mainly as a result of the uninhibited issue of Lloyds' bonds. The only option available was the sale of the railway's plant and equipment to help meet the outstanding debts. By now Mr Holden had moved his contractor's plant from the Llandyssil line to Kidwelly. When he found that some of his items were at risk of being included in the sale he promptly objected. He also argued that equipment paid for out of the separate Kidwelly branch funds should be exempt, and the C&CR Board acknowledged the point. Unfortunately amongst the equipment included in the sale were two locomotives recently purchased from Rothwell & Co., and all the rolling stock. When the sale took place in February 1865, agreements were made with the buyers to hire this stock back in order to maintain a service on the line. Two other locomotives were already on hire from the builders, Sharp, Stewart & Co., but during 1865 these were re-possessed for a time.

In March 1865 it was reported that John Everitt 'the intended Receiver' would no longer be so because of the large amount of security required by the Court of Chancery. Instead, the Directors invited him to become Managing Director! In the event he refused, so the Board invited him to investigate the position of the company and to attend their meetings. It was also agreed that he should be entrusted with one of the keys to the company seal to demonstrate their good faith in undertaking not to increase the company's liabilities without his sanction. On 2nd May, 1865, he advised the Directors that over £50,000 in Lloyds' bonds were held by Mr Holden, and urged them to press for particulars of Mr Holden's account, and to refuse to transfer any bonds, stocks, or securities to other parties on Holden's behalf.

This advice caused a new crisis. By the spring of 1865 Mr Holden was at work on the construction of the Kidwelly branches, and was expecting to be paid whenever an engineer's certificate of work done was passed to the company. Meanwhile in May, Lloyds' bonds issued five years earlier to John Jay, the original contractor, matured. According to the company's understanding with its current contractor, Holden should have bought the lot and returned them to the company. In the event he could only find £4,000 of the £21,500 required, and so applied to the company for the difference. In effect he was inviting the company to increase its liabilities, and Everitt promptly objected, refusing access to his key to the company seal. The Board rescinded their decision to allow him a key, but by now matters were going from bad to dreadful. Creditors seemed to be appearing at every turn, and by the beginning of July the Chairman of the Carmarthen & Cardigan, J.L. Propert, had received writs from both Jay and Holden.

In spite of problems of payment, Holden appears to have persevered with his contract until September. On 1st June, 1865, the *Llanelly & County Guardian* carried the following report under the heading 'Gwendraeth Valley and Kidwelly Railway':

The contractors are now busily engaged in the construction of these lines upwards of 120 men being at present employed. It is impossible to over-estimate the importance of these lines, as by their aid the whole of the mineral wealth of the central portion of Carmarthenshire will be rendered accessible, and the public will reap the benefit in a reduction of the prices of coal and lime. The Carway branch is about seven miles long, and will run to the Carway colliery belonging to Mr Owen Bowen, close to the pit's mouth, so that the colliers can tip the coal into the railway cars without delay, and thus materially reduce the cost of transit. The terminus will be at Pontyberem, where there are extensive iron works and collieries. We trust that in the course of the summer the work will be well forwarded.

There is some irony in this report in that the Act authorising the construction of the coal line to Carway and Pontyberem was not passed by Parliament until

29th June, 1865. Cited as the C&CR (Kidwelly Extension) Act, it provided for two sections of railway, built either to the broad gauge or with a mixed gauge. The first railway was to run from Kidwelly to a field in the hamlet of Glyn 'belonging to the Trustees of the late Colonel Francis Charles James Pemberton, and in the occupation of the Carway & Duffryn Steam Coal Company Limited'. The second railway was the extension north from Carway to a terminus 'near the Pontyberrem Coal and Iron Works in the Parish of Llanon and Hamlet of Glyn.') One interesting feature of the Act was a clause included primarily for the protection of the Kidwelly & Llanelly Canal. This stated:

> The bridge to be constructed . . . for carrying the Railway hereby authorised over Kymer's Canal shall be of such dimensions as to admit of a double line of rails on the Narrow Gauge, being constructed under the said bridge, and to admit of the passage of engines and carriages upon the said lines of railway; and the width of the said bridge over the said canal shall therefore be not less than twenty feet, measured on the square between the abutments; and the clear height of the bridge throughout shall be not less than fifteen feet . . .

On this occasion five years were allowed for the completion of the railways authorised by the Act, and powers were granted for the creation of an additional £70,000 of Kidwelly Branch shares, and for borrowing a further £23,000 on mortgage.

In the event Holden never managed to build a bridge over what had originally been Kymer's Canal, but there is no doubt that despite the financial problems and limited resources, Holden achieved a remarkable amount at Kidwelly in 1864 and 1865. When questioned on the subject a year later, the Engineer John Wright described the work in this way: 'Commencing at Kidwelly all the junctions with the South Wales are completed. There are some branches also completed down to the canal about a mile and a half of permanent way laid, and works, in all for about three miles and a half'. He added that about 47 acres of land had been purchased for the purpose, and as regards the coal line 'about half a mile of that is done'.

If John Wright considered that the coal line commenced at the junction with the South Wales main line his estimated length was broadly accurate. The earthworks for the coal line petered out in the fields alongside the Kidwelly & Llanelly Canal, and whilst it appears that the railway was to be carried on a wooden trestle over a small stream to run alongside the canal bank, only a few piles for the trestle were sunk. In contrast, the earthworks for the lime line reached way beyond Mynydd-y-Garreg, almost to Llechdwnni. A recent field survey revealed that these earthworks had been very substantial, and indeed worthy of a main line. The generous dimensions clearly indicated accommodation for broad gauge track, and far greater expense than would have been incurred in the construction of a standard gauge route. The limit of these works was near the top of a long steady gradient in the vicinity of a farm named Gledwyn. This the line skirted by a magnificent, slightly curved embankment containing an architecturally pleasing single arched bridge about 25 ft high. The embankment carried the line into a deep rock cutting north of Gledwyn, terminating at a quarry-like rock face. Nineteenth century maps

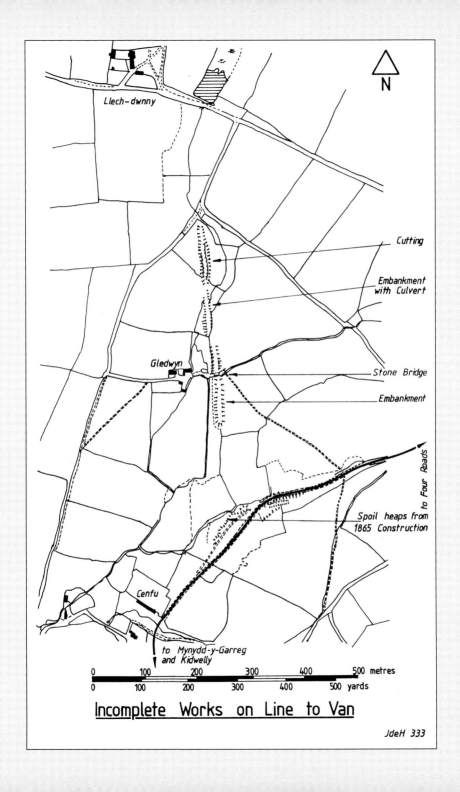

Llech-dwnny

Cutting

Embankment
with Culvert

Gledwyn

Stone Bridge

Embankment

to Four Roads

Spoil heaps from
1865 Construction

Cenfu

to Mynydd-y-Garreg
and Kidwelly

| 0 | 100 | 200 | 300 | 400 | 500 metres |
| 0 | 100 | 200 | 300 | 400 | 500 yards |

Incomplete Works on Line to Van

JdeH 333

The abandoned trackbed of the 'Lime Line', looking south towards Mynydd-y-Garreg. This portion of the trackbed was used later by the standard gauge Young's line from Penymynydd.
Author

The bridge beneath the uncompleted 'Lime Line' at Gledwyn Farm, near Llech-dwnny, north of Mynydd-y-Garreg. *Author*

The round-arched underbridge under the unfinished Carmarthen & Cardigan broad gauge 'Lime Line' at Gledwyn Farm. *Author*

suggest that the ground between this point and the nearby country lane at Llechdwnni may have been disturbed, but study of the site today is inconclusive.

On the basis of Wright's statement it may be assumed that the permanent way was laid to the road crossing at what was later known as Minkie Road, and that the remainder of the route to Mynydd-y-Garreg was ready to receive it. The reference to 'branches' to the canal implies that even at this early date a branch was being built at Kidwelly from the junction with the South Wales main line to the Kidwelly & Llanelly Canal at Tycoch, even though not specifically referred to in the authorising Act of Parliament.

By this stage the Receiver was a Mr Howe, and he now intervened to take direct control of the company. He may have felt that the situation that confronted him was so messy it was impossible to know whom to trust. At all events the stage was set for a palace revolution. The Receiver appointed his son, Samuel Howe, as General Manager, who had no hesitation in exercising his new found powers. He quickly sacked most of the staff and recruited a number of others whom the Directors regarded as inexperienced. On 14th August, 1865, the C&CR Board met at their customary venue, 4 Chatham Place, Blackfriars, London, under the chairmanship of J.L. Propert, for the last time. One Director had already resigned, and two new appointments made, and other long standing Board members were far from happy. Before long there were more resignations and more replacements, and when the Board met next on 19th September it had an entirely new complexion. Only J.L. Propert and Samuel Crosse from the old team remained as Directors, and most significant of all, the energetic Owen Bowen had resigned as company Secretary. Although too little is known of Bowen's career and interests, it is difficult to think that his departure was a loss to the C&CR. His commercial achievements may suggest ability, but the chequered career of the railway company implies either incompetence or a lack of integrity, or both. Latterly Bowen was undoubtedly involved in the dishonest and disastrous dealings with Lloyds' bonds, and he may well have committed other misdemeanours. Some years later Bowen's reputation took a further knock when mismanagement of the Carway colliery caused the landowners to give Bowen's company notice to quit.

The first task confronting the new Board was to restore some order to the Carmarthen & Cardigan's appalling finances. In late September and early October the Directors, or sub-committees of Directors, were meeting in London several times each week in their effort to get a grip on the situation. A sub-committee meeting on 28th September was typical. A new Director, Joseph Ivimey, was Chairman, assisted by the new company Secretary, Frederick Edwards. The meeting agreed upon a thorough investigation of the issue of Lloyds' bonds, and resolved that no further transfers of Lloyds' bonds would be registered pending the outcome of the investigation.

At numerous moments in the ensuing days the Board acknowledged that they needed Owen Bowen's assistance to make some sense of the mess - but it is not at all clear that they got it. Meanwhile, at a meeting on 3rd October, a letter was received from the company accountant, Alexander Young, begging for 'something on account of his salary'. Payment of £10 was authorised! At the same meeting the Secretary submitted a scheme devised by a Mr Eaglesfield to reconstruct the capital of the company.

By 7th October the Directors must have felt that they had learned enough about their contractor, H.A. Holden, and he was given formal notice of the termination of his contracts. A few days later a row broke out about 10,000 sleepers stored in a timber yard at Llanelly docks. Apparently Holden had asked the company to pay for them some time earlier, and the appropriate bonds had been issued. On these facts Frederick Edwards was told to go to Llanelly to obtain possession. On his arrival he learned that a Mr Rosser, a surveyor who had done work for the company, had claimed 2,792 sleepers, and had taken possession, allegedly on the authority of Owen Bowen! Furthermore, the owner of the timber yard declared that he held the remaining sleepers on behalf of Mr Holden, and wanted Mr Holden's authority to release them. Just to add to the woes of the company Secretary, the sleepers were not stacked properly, and there was some suspicion of pilfering! Within a couple of days Mr Edwards reported by telegram that the sleepers had been seized by a C&CR creditor. Accordingly he had to come home empty-handed, and a solicitor was left with the wretched job of trying to reclaim them for the company.

Whilst this little episode was being played out in South Wales, creditors were producing more bills and bonds for payment. By late October the frustrated C&CR Board - apparently with the support of the Receiver, Mr Howe - was reduced to disregarding the claims of some bond holders on the grounds that they were invalid. Meanwhile, Mr Howe himself was studying plans of the C&CR, and looking to the future. On 24th October Mr Wright, the Engineer, submitted plans and sections of the Kidwelly lime line, showing also 'the proposed deviation of line by Mr Blathwayte'. Mr Blathwayte was a surveyor then resident at the Pelican Inn at Kidwelly; regrettably no details have come to light regarding the proposed deviation in relation to the original route. What is clear is that the C&CR urgently needed an Act of Parliament creating a new company to control the Kidwelly branches. The reason was put succinctly at a Board meeting held in December: 'It will be impossible to resume construction of the branches until they are made free from the [C&C] main line debts'. At this moment it was still supposed that both the coal line and the lime line would be built; accordingly it seemed reasonable to give the new company the title of the Gwendraeth Valleys Railway.

A new Bill was duly drafted, but when the bondholders and creditors became aware of it, some expressed considerable disquiet. Most of the bonds were now in the hands of two finance companies, represented on the new C&CR Board by a Mr Crawford and a Dr Collum. Edward Threlfall from Cheshire held £5,000 worth of bonds, for which he claimed to have given full value. On 15th February, 1866, he was sufficiently concerned by developments to ask the C&CR that the new company be made to accept the same liability as the C&C in respect of his bonds. This was not what the Bill's promoters had in mind, as the main object of the exercise was to free the Kidwelly branches of old liabilities. Instead it was proposed that shares in the new company should be issued in place of bonds. Threlfall was invited to accept this arrangement (as the two finance companies had done) or risk getting nothing.

   Threlfall's response was to oppose the Bill, and attend the House of Lords' committee taking evidence on the Bill in early June 1866.   In this setting he claimed to have acquired the bonds from Holden as part payment in a property transaction involving five plots of building land at Tranmere, Birkenhead. Whatever value he and Holden put upon them, Frederick Edwards, after reference to company papers, declared 'you do not appear to have advanced even 50 per cent upon the Bonds you hold'.   Given the state of the C&CR's books, the reliability of this assertion (and several others made by Edwards) was open to question. However the main concern of the House of Lords was to put the new company on a proper footing, and late in June it approved the Bill on the condition that satisfactory security could be given for the completion of the Kidwelly branches. The Act received the Royal Assent on 30th July, 1866, and after this long and troublesome pregnancy, the Gwendraeth Valleys Railway was born.

ANNO VICESIMO NONO & TRICESIMO

VICTORIÆ REGINÆ.

****

Cap. ccxcvii.

An Act to separate the *Kidwelly* Branch and
Extension from the rest of the Undertaking of
the *Carmarthen and Cardigan* Railway Company,
and to incorporate a Company for the Purposes
of the said Branch and Extension.
                              [30th *July* 1866.]

WHEREAS by " The *Carmarthen and Cardigan* Railway   27 & 28 Vict.
(*Kidwelly* Branch) Act, 1864," Power is given to the   c. xiii.
Carmarthen and Cardigan Railway Company (Section 8)
to raise additional Capital amounting to One hundred thousand
Pounds by the Creation of new Shares in their Undertaking, and it is
provided by the same Act that the said Shares should form a separate
Capital, to be termed " *Carmarthen and Cardigan* (*Kidwelly* Branch)
Shares," and might have assigned to them exclusively, or in certain
definite Proportions, the net Profits of the Railway authorized by the
said Act, to the Exclusion or partial Exclusion of Participation of
Profits in the rest of the Company's Undertaking; and by the 11th
Section of the same Act Provision is made for keeping separate
Accounts ; and it is also provided that it should not be lawful for the
Holders of the new Capital to interfere with the general Affairs of
[*Local.*]   49 *H*   the

Chapter Four

The Broad Gauge and After

The career of the GVR as a broad gauge line appears to have been brief and not very successful. The presence of Owen Bowen's limekilns at Mynydd-y-Garreg almost certainly generated some freight for the railway in the form of coal to the kilns and lime away from them. Meanwhile at Kidwelly two recently opened brickworks probably contributed useful traffic, whilst the short branch constructed alongside the South Wales main line to a wharf on the Kidwelly & Llanelly Canal at Tycoch may well have been even more productive. According to a document drafted in 1875, 'up to the year 1868 the said wharf was largely used for the purpose of traffic passing between the GVR and the said canal, and thence to Kidwelly Quay, Burry Port and other places in connection therewith'.

By an Act of 1865 the Kidwelly & Llanelly Canal Co. became known as the Kidwelly & Burry Port Railway Co., with powers to discontinue all or part of the canal and replace it with railways. In the following year this undertaking changed its name again to become the Burry Port & Gwendraeth Valley Railway (BP&GVR) clearly implying that the future lay with railways. However, the idea of converting the canal in this way was not new: as early as March 1862, the C&CR had contemplated the possibility of purchasing the canal for this purpose, instructing its engineer's Messrs Cubitt & Wright to make a preliminary survey. Suffice to say that it was not until 1868 that the plans of the BP&GVR had advanced sufficiently to begin the conversion of the canal into a railway. In the words of the 1875 document,

> ... during the execution of the said works the communication between the GVR and the said canal was of necessity interrupted. On the completion of the works it was found that the level of the rails of the said railway [the BP&GVR] as constructed was considerably lower than the level of the water as it stood in the canal previous to the construction of the said railway.

Put another way, the link between the two concerns was severed, and as the new BP&GV line was built to the standard gauge of 4 ft 8½ in. it could not be restored.

The canal was last used in August 1868, and its closure must have had an impact on the GVR's frail finances. Some traffic would have been lost to road carters, and some would have been routed over the South Wales main line from Burry Port. Although there are no figures available for any remaining traffic, it is unlikely to have been enough to sustain the company for very long. On the basis of slight circumstantial evidence, it seems likely that the broad gauge GVR simply expired in 1869. According to a newspaper report of April 1872, the railway had then 'been at a standstill for a considerable time'.

Unfortunately no company papers for this critical period have come to light, and it is not entirely clear who was in command. The Act of 1866 required the GVR to have a minimum of four and a maximum of six Directors, with a quorum of three, and by it four members of the C&CR Board were named as

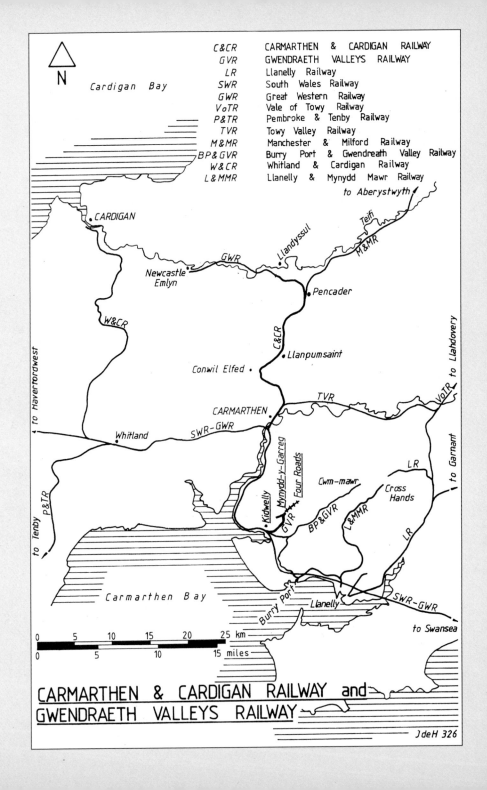

CARMARTHEN & CARDIGAN RAILWAY and GWENDRAETH VALLEYS RAILWAY

Directors of the Gwendraeth Valleys, James H. Crawford, Robert Collum, William Parsons and Joseph Ivimey. By 1870 only the last two were recorded as Directors, so quite how the company conducted its business in these circumstances is something of a mystery. Even so, it must be assumed that those responsible were taking note of the overall course of events in South Wales. By this time it was becoming clear that the days of Brunel's broad gauge in the area were numbered. The BP&GVR and the much earlier Llanelly Railway were built to the standard gauge, and if the South Wales main line was altered, both the GVR and the Carmarthen & Cardigan would be obliged to make their lines compatible with those of their neighbours. The cost must have been a matter of increasing concern to both companies.

The need to raise new capital for the Gwendraeth Valleys line and associated industries was obvious, and even before the closure of the broad gauge GVR an attempt was made to do this. In February 1868, the Gwendraeth Valleys Lime, Coal and Railway Co. was formed. Its declared objects included 'purchasing or leasing . . . any railway or canal in that district'. Reference was also made to the working and burning of limestone, the acquisition of collieries, and the hire or sale of rolling stock of railways, quarries, collieries, canals and the like. The nominal capital was £100,00 in 5,000 £20 shares. The recorded subscribers had addresses in London and South-East England, and included a railway engineer, James H. Shipway of Westminster, and a railway contractor, Edward Humphreys, also of Westminster. By March 1869, 185 shares had been taken up, but 110 had been forfeited. Only £1,320 had been received in respect of the remaining shares. The company was wound up by Court order on 30th December, 1869.

Even before this company had been buried, another had been born with almost identical aims. The Kidwelly Railway, Lime and Colliery Co. was registered on 21st September, 1869, with another list of subscribers from London and South-East England, one of whom, Thomas Hutchings of Lewisham, was described as a railway contractor. The nominal capital was £150,000 in 7,500 £20 shares, but by January 1870 only 35 shares had been taken up and £700 received. On 21st July, 1870, a special resolution was passed (and confirmed a month later) stating 'that taking into consideration the difficulties that have arisen through Mr Eaglesfield declining to carry out his contract, and the want of funds successfully to carry on litigation against him, this company now be dissolved'. Although Mr Eaglesfield is known to have had some financial involvement with the Carmarthen & Cardigan Railway in the painful 1860s, no more is said in this context of the contract mentioned. However the Chairman of the meeting at which the resolution was passed was none other than H.A. Holden. Here, surely, is a clue to what was happening. In the Carmarthen & Cardigan era at Kidwelly a number of people had suffered loss through their involvement. The brief attempts to find fresh capital to complete the works at Kidwelly were probably weak efforts to make good some of the loss incurred. Both failed utterly, but a third company formed soon after did much better.

The Mynydd-y-Garreg and Kidwelly Railway and Lime Co. was incorporated on 10th August, 1871, with a nominal capital of £50,000 in £10 shares. Its objects were stated to include the completion of the works of the

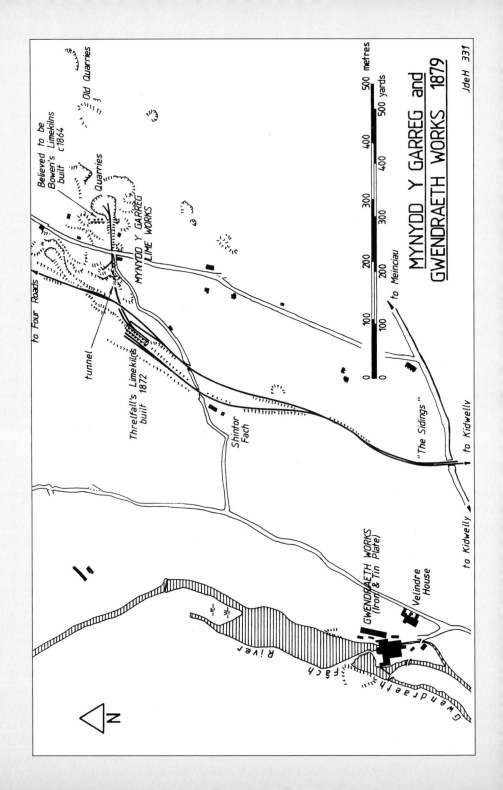

MYNYDD Y GARREG and
GWENDRAETH WORKS 1879

JdeH 331

Carmarthen & Cardigan Railway, although without specific reference to colliery acquisition.

The registered office of the new company was in Manchester, and the subscribers, bar one, gave addresses in North-West England; three of them were cotton spinners. The one London subscriber was Edward Threlfall, gentleman of Kensington, described in another company document as 'railway manager of Kidwelly, South Wales'. On this basis it would seem that Threlfall had emerged from the turmoil of the preceding years to gain control of the sickly undertaking, and with the aid of friends and associates from the North-West hoped to restore both the company and his own investment by the raising of new capital.

This picture is supported by a report in the *Llanelly Guardian* for 11th April, 1872, which was especially concerned to describe the construction of more limekilns at Mynydd-y-Garreg:

> The Kidwelly and Mynydd Garreg [*sic*] lime railway has been purchased by Mr Threlfall, and it is now in a fair way towards completion. On Saturday the ceremony of laying the foundations of new limekilns in connection with the railway was performed, after an agreeable introductory speech by Mr Jacob Chivers, Velindre, by Miss Threlfall, and was witnessed by a large concourse of people. A cold collation was partaken of by over 200 persons, including the employees. The weather was exceedingly favourable. Alderman Thomas addressed the assemblage. The bells from the tower of old St Mary's rang many peals at intervals in honour of the day's festivities.

Four weeks later the same newspaper mentioned the start of work on the conversion of the South Wales main line from the broad gauge to the standard gauge. The task took three weeks to complete, with a good deal of disruption to regular services; as the GVR was not operating a service the company was not under pressure to conform to everyone else's timetable for the work. Even so, they pressed on with relaying or regauging the track, and by the autumn the job was done. On 31st October, 1872, under the heading 'Mynydd-y-Garreg Lime Works', the *Llanelly Guardian* stated: 'The line of railway to these works is now ready for traffic. Dr Percy, of the Royal School of Mines, and Dr Rosser, Owen's College, Manchester, have analysed the limestone and declared that it contains from 96.04 per cent to 98.47 per cent of carbonate of lime, and is equal to any for agricultural and other purposes'.

Additional capital was undoubtedly needed. During 1871 it became known that the South Wales main line would be converted to the standard gauge compelling the GVR to be rebuilt to the same gauge. In addition the GVR needed to make a new connection with the BP&GVR at Tycoch, east of Kidwelly. For this purpose additional land at Tycoch was acquired in August and December 1872. More land, mostly small strips and corners of property along the rest of the GVR, were purchased in 1872 and 1873. Although this was done in the name of the GVR, it is not clear how it was all financed. By the end of 1872 the newly formed Mynydd-y-Garreg & Kidwelly Railway & Lime Co. had only 220 shares taken up, and even as late as October 1877, only 761 shares were fully paid up. Presumably certain supporters contributed privately, without receiving shares or any other acknowledgment for it.

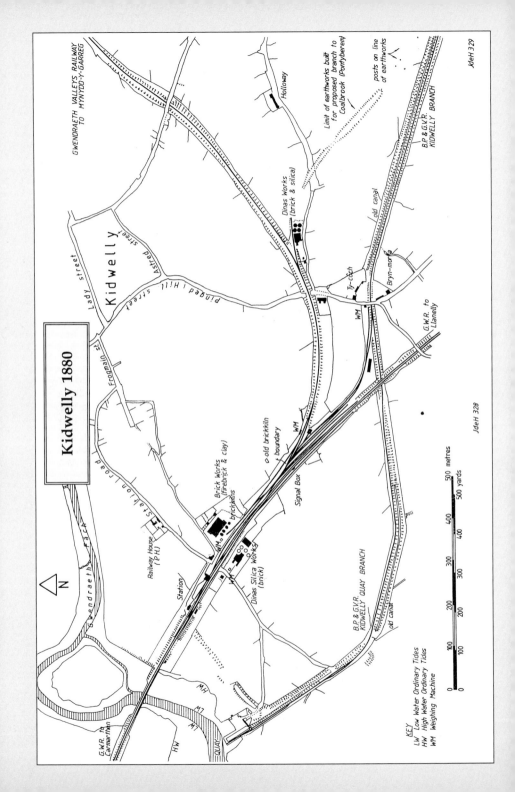

Kidwelly 1880

N

GWENDRAETH VALLEYS RAILWAY
TO MYNYDD-Y-GARREG

Kidwelly

Lady street

Astreet

Pinged Hill street

Frogmain st.

Station Road

Holloway

Dinas Works
(brick & silica)

Limit of earthworks built
for proposed branch to
Coalbrook (Pontyberem)

posts on line
of earthworks

JdeH 329

B.P. & G.V.R.
KIDWELLY BRANCH

old canal

Ty-côch

Bryn-mor

WM

G.W.R. to
Llanelly

WM

Signal Box

Brick Works
(firebrick & clay)

old brickkiln

boundary

brickpaths

old canal

B.P. & G.V.R.
KIDWELLY QUAY BRANCH

JdeH 328

Railway House
(P.H.)

WM

Dinas Silica Works
(brick)

WM

Station

Gwendraeth Fach

G.W.R. to
Carmarthen

MH

MT

HW

QUAY

HW

500 metres

500 yards

0	100	200	300	400	
0	100	200	300	400	

KEY
LW Low Water Ordinary Tides
HW High Water Ordinary Tides
WM Weighing Machine

Although this new company was clearly in control of the GVR, and made land purchases in its own name, it appears to have allowed the railway to trade as the Gwendraeth Valleys Railway. The precise date of the opening of the GVR as a standard gauge line is not known, but in view of the newspaper report already mentioned a date in October or November 1872 seems highly likely. Track was laid to the quarries and limekilns at Mynydd-y-Garreg, but not beyond. No attempt was made to revive 'the coal line', although a siding was provided at the site of the junction of this line to serve the Dinas Silica Brickworks now located at this spot. The short section to Tycoch was converted to the standard gauge a little later, and a connection with the BP&GVR was opened in September 1873. Although the new junction shortened the route for traffic to and from Kidwelly and the west by about nine miles, and reduced costs, the BP&GV disliked the arrangement, probably because it reduced the number of miles freight moved over its line, and so reduced its income.

According to a GVR document, the attitude of the BP&GVR became thoroughly unhelpful. It seems that traffic was forwarded to Tycoch at erratic and unpredictable times, and sometimes only once or twice a week. Inevitably through traffic was often delayed for long periods, generating complaints to the GVR and a good deal of frustration for the management. For some time the problems at Tycoch soured relations between the two companies, and the situation deteriorated further when the BP&GVR threatened to remove the junction altogether. In 1875 the GVR decided that traffic had been obstructed for long enough, and so referred the dispute to the Railway Commissioners for a ruling under the Regulation of Railways Act, 1873. The outcome went in favour of the GVR, but there appears to have been an element of compromise in that soon after an arrangement was reached whereby the Burry Port company became responsible for working the GVR. This was formalised by an agreement between the two companies dated 30th November, 1876 (see Appendix One), as a result of which the GVR's only locomotive was taken into BP&GV stock.

In reality the GVR was probably poorly placed to argue with the Burry Port company. From 1875 there was a protracted economic slump which, although affecting both companies, may well have hurt the smaller company more. In 1877 the GVR was said to be virtually bankrupt, but to keep the line open somehow persuaded the GWR to make an allowance on its traffic rates of either 2d./ton or 1d./ton, depending on the type of traffic. In 1878, according to one source, the GVR failed to pay interest on its debentures.

Even in a difficult economic climate there are a few people willing to make a new investment. In 1876 one such was Alexander Young. Although no evidence is to hand, he may well have been one and the same as the Alexander Young who served the C&CR as its accountant in the painful 1860s. If so, his acquaintance with the railway may have made him aware of the mineral wealth of Mynydd-y-Garreg and district. Given an apparent family involvement with the silica brick industry (referred to in Chapter Seven) it would seem that he decided to invest in it for himself. The fact that he chose to make his investment at Penymynydd Farm, Four Roads, has given rise to a suggestion that he may in some way have been related to the Brigstocke family of Llechdwnni, who owned much of the land around Penymynydd. However it seems more likely that he favoured this site because it was outside the Kidwelly Corporation lands at Mynydd-y-Garreg.

At all events, in or about 1876 he opened a stone quarry, and then built five limekilns in an impressive block alongside the lane from Penymynydd Farm to Graig and Mynydd-y-Garreg. Built in dressed stone, and standing over 30 ft high, these kilns were a great improvement on the smaller farmers' kilns dotted about the Mynydd-y-Garreg limestone district. Young's ambitions extended beyond the local agricultural trade, and he obtained the landowners' permission to build his own private standard gauge railway from Mynydd-y-Garreg to Penymynydd Farm, a distance of 1½ miles. The old C&CR trackbed was available for about half the route, and most of the remainder is thought to have been over Brigstocke estate land. It is believed that this line was ready for traffic at or very soon after the completion and opening of the limekilns in 1877.

In the same year, 1877, the proprietor of the Kidwelly Tinplate works, Jacob Chivers, decided to hand over the business to his son, Thomas, and concentrate on his industrial interests at Cinderford in the Forest of Dean. Evidently Thomas was an optimist, because he gained £15,000 by mortgage and began a programme of expansion. In 1879 he began to build an 'upper' works, north of his existing premises, and installed six new tin mills to add to the three already in use at the original site. By 1882 all nine were in use, by which time Thomas Chivers had also provided new workmen's cottages at Mynydd-y-Garreg, and at Gwendraeth Town, on the northern side of Kidwelly. Transport improvements were not neglected, and in 1879 land was acquired at Mynydd-y-Garreg for the construction of a short branch railway from the 1872 limekilns back into the tinplate works; at the same period the limekilns appear to have become the property of the Mynydd-y-Garreg & Kidwelly Railway & Lime Co. A survey of this location, undertaken in April 1879, revealed no sign of the new branch being built, but it is thought that the work was tackled later in the same year, with the new connection being operational by 1880. Sadly no official records have yet come to light to show the benefits of this new source of railway traffic, but it may have been a factor in the preparation of a revised working agreement between the GVR and the BP&GVR in 1883.

Incidental evidence of an increase in business was given in a newspaper report of 29th November, 1883, in relation to an accident on the Great Western Railway at Kidwelly. At about 4.30 am on a wet Saturday morning an engine driver was working alone on shunting duties on the up side of the main line. In the darkness it seems that neither he nor the signalman were aware that a few empty wagons had run out onto the up main line. Clear signals were given to an express from Neyland, which soon arrived at speed and smashed the wagons to pieces. Mercifully no one was seriously hurt, 'but the damage to rolling stock was estimated . . . at something like £5,000'. The newspaper clearly hinted that the railway staff had been working excessive hours, noting that 'there has been great pressure of traffic in the Kidwelly goods department in consequence of the activity of the tin, brick and lime works of the district, which are connected by small branch lines'. Plainly the source of much of this traffic, the Gwendraeth Valleys Railway, was now no longer simply the 'lime line', but a company with widening industrial interests.

Chapter Five

The Manchester Era, 1884-1904

When Edward Threlfall won control of the Gwendraeth Valleys Railway, and became the prime-mover in the formation of the Mynydd-y-Garreg & Kidwelly Railway & Lime Co., the registered office for the new company was set up in Manchester, a location convenient for Threlfall's friends and business associates who were backing his enterprise. Charles and George Lings were cotton spinners; John Hall of Bramall Lodge, Stockport, was described variously as a cotton spinner and a silversmith; George E. Hardman of Haslingden was a merchant; William Slater of Burnage a solicitor, and Richard Roberts, also of Burnage, was an insurance agent. On the face of it, the involvement of these men in the story of the GVR would appear to parallel the involvement of the McConnel family in the early history of the Talyllyn Railway. The McConnels were proprietors of a large cotton mill in Manchester, and when the American Civil War cut off supplies of raw cotton for spinning they decided to diversify their interests. In 1864 they formed the Aberdovey Slate Co. to work the Bryn Eglwys quarry at Abergynolwyn, and planned a railway to link it with the coast. By the time the 2 ft 3 in. gauge Talyllyn Railway was opened, in December 1866, the war in North America was over, and cotton imports had resumed.

In somewhat similar fashion, Edward Threlfall made his investment in or about 1864, and quickly became entangled in the chaos which so hampered the Carmarthen & Cardigan Railway. No doubt he regretted his involvement, but plainly he was a fighter, and willing to go on taking some risks. He must also have been blessed with considerable powers of persuasion, because most of his friends and colleagues stayed with him in the Mynydd-y-Garreg and Kidwelly Railway & Lime Co. through the difficulties of the 1870s, and by October 1877, when 761 shares had been taken up, the shareholders' list comprised Edward and Mary Threlfall, John Hall, Charles and George Lings, G.E. Hardman, William Slater, Lord Clarence Paget, John T. Emmerson, J.D. Carter, H. Hoyle, and the Executors of the late J. Smethurst. This list was virtually unchanged in 1887, in which year the registered office was moved to Westminster Buildings, 35 Brown Street, Manchester.

Unfortunately no very detailed records have come to light relating to either the Railway & Lime Co., or the GVR, prior to 1884. The former always appears to have been the dominant concern, taking the major decisions; the earliest available minute book for the Gwendraeth Valleys Railway begins late in 1884, but even then the minutes are brief and uninformative. At this time the Chairman of the GVR was John Hall, and his fellow Directors were William Slater, Edward Threlfall and George Turner Hardman. The last named was newly appointed to replace his father, G.E. Hardman, who had died a few months before. In similar fashion, when John Hall died on 20th August, 1887, he was succeeded by his son, John Henry Hall. William Slater succeeded as company Chairman; the company auditor was John White. GVR Board

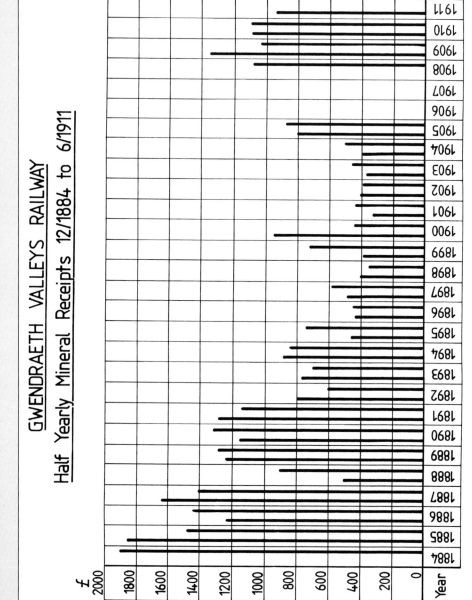

GWENDRAETH VALLEYS RAILWAY

Half Yearly Mineral Receipts 12/1884 to 6/1911

JdeH 339

meetings were held at 37 Brown Street, Manchester, the business address of an accountant, George Williamson, who was the company Secretary.

The half-yearly reports of the GVR Directors are marginally more helpful than the minute books. Even so, there is no reference at all to a dispute between Alexander Young and the Gwendraeth Valleys Railway over freight rates and what were described as 'terminal services'. In 1885 this dispute went to the Railway Commissioners, and judgement was given in favour of Young. The 'terminal charges' were regarded as unwarrantable, and certain wayleave tolls had to be amended. As this outcome must have been a burden to the GVR, it is somewhat surprising that it does not appear to have been mentioned. In later years the Directors did not hesitate to refer to their difficulties, not least the fluctuating traffic to and from Kidwelly Tinplate Works.

In the 1880s trading conditions were adverse for many industries, and tinplate had its share of problems, not least because over-production by numerous firms had caused a drop in prices. At Kidwelly Thomas Chivers was in serious trouble, and for a time could not meet his bills with several traders, including the Burry Port & Gwendraeth Valley Railway. His plight created considerable difficulties for the GVR also. During the winter of 1885/6 Chivers asked his workmen to take a cut in wages, and they refused. Accordingly, in February 1886, he gave 28 days notice of his intention to terminate contracts. Work came to a halt on the expiry of the notice, and although it has been said that production was halted for fully five months, this is not supported precisely by the GVR Directors' report for the six months to 30th June, 1886. In this document it was noted that: 'On account of the stoppage for several months of Mr Chivers' works the traffic has been very much decreased. These works have again started, and the Directors hope they will so continue'.

The essential fact was that tinplate production resumed, at least for a while. At the same period there was some good news from the silica brick industry. The Kidwelly R. Dinas Fire Brick Company was incorporated on 3rd September, 1886, with an authorised capital of £20,000 in £1 shares. Its purpose was to take over George Redford's business, which had been trading as the R. Dinas Fire Brick & Silicate Works. Although an intention was expressed to issue 3,500 shares in the new company to Redford, by January 1887 a Mrs Mary Fitzgerald of London was easily the largest subscriber with some 700 shares out of 712 then issued. Shareholders with but one share included Redford, John Coley Bromford, a London engineer, and Walter Fitzgerald, the company Secretary. According to an agreement made on 16th December, 1887, the then existing rights and interests of Redford and Coley Bromford were to cease, allowing the new company to carry on the business. In addition two acres of land vested in Henry Smart (believed to be one and the same as Henry Smart, manager of the GVR) was to be sold to the Fire Brick Co. This must have comprised most of the works' site, because the sale was to include 'the engine, steam engine, and all other plant and machines in or about the premises'. Smart himself had an interest in the silica sand and stone business, having leased 7½ acres of Mynydd-y-Garreg from Kidwelly Corporation for this purpose in 1881; it seems entirely possible that he worked collaboratively with the Kidwelly R. Dinas Fire Brick Co.

Before this centre of the silica brick industry had fully reshaped itself, the Kidwelly Tinplate Works was again in crisis. Now Thomas Chivers' problems were not just serious, but dire, as he faced an even wider range of creditors seeking payment. In the autumn of 1887 Chivers leased 10 wagons from the BP&GVR who unwisely allowed the arrangement to take effect without putting anything in writing. The wagons were soon reclaimed, but no money was ever received in respect of them. By December John Russell, the Receiver of the BP&GVR was so exasperated with Chivers' behaviour that he gave directions that any goods belonging to Chivers in the care of the BP&GV should be detained to set against outstanding transport costs of £117 8s. 9d. In pursuance of this policy, the BP&GV on 12th December detained no less than 36 wagons loaded with Chivers' tinplate, although Russell (ever the gentleman!) agreed that the wagons' contents should be made available to the creditors as a whole. This was just as well, because some of Chivers' other debts were far larger. The GVR was owed £714 9s. 5d., and Bolitho & Sons, the Cornish tin smelters, were owed £2246 19s. The Ebbw Vale company, Chivers' chief source of iron, was either generous or inept in its credit controls, because they were owed a massive £7,892!

For Chivers, this financial crisis was the last straw. Production stopped abruptly in December 1887, and he was obliged to put the business up for sale. Early in 1888 he opened negotiations with some prominent local businessmen, including David Evans of Llangennech, and Dr Henry Child Buckley of Llanelli. As a result the works changed hands for £25,000, and Chivers' mortgage to the National Provincial Bank was redeemed. A new company was formed named the Gwendraeth Tinplate Co. Ltd, with a Board of Directors including Evans, Buckley, J. Beavan Phillips, David Paton, and also Thomas Chivers. Production resumed, although the GVR Directors' report for the period to 31st December, 1888 noted that 'the works of the Gwendraeth Tinplate Co. Ltd are not yet turning out their full amount of goods, and consequently the traffic returns were not so satisfactory as the Directors expected'. No doubt relieved by the change of management, John Russell of the BP&GV signed a traffic agreement with the new company on 30th June, 1888.

The year 1889 saw a significant improvement in traffic, and the receipts for the half-year to the end of June were more than double those for the equivalent period in the preceding year. A major concern for the Directors was generating enough income to pay the interest due on the company's debentures, mortgage bonds and loans. In June 1889 they expressed the hope that in a short time revenue would have 'so improved as to enable them to meet regularly the interest accruing'. The reality was that these payments were often made late, and in spite of the hopes expressed by the GVR Directors matters did not improve. Indeed it is believed that in 1891 the railway simply failed to pay any debenture interest, increasing the irritation of debenture holders, and precipitating legal action. The Directors' half-yearly report, at the end of June 1892, declared that the company's financial problems were a consequence of 'the Tin Plate Trade in South Wales having been in such an unsettled condition'. Six months later the Directors reported that they had paid three months interest on the debentures, but that in the last half year traffic had decreased 'to such an extent that no further payment could be made'. For the debenture holders this news was probably the last straw, but one had already put the GVR under pressure to such an extent that the Directors had been compelled to apply to the Court of Chancery for the appointment of a Receiver, 'so as to protect the assets of the company, and to carry on the railway in the usual way'. The Receiver appointed was the GVR company Secretary, George Williamson.

The Directors' reference to the unsettled state of the tinplate industry was entirely justified. Indeed, the word 'unsettled' was nothing if not an understatement! The main reason for the crisis in the industry lay far beyond South Wales. Prior to 1891 the United States provided a market for about three-quarters of the entire British output of tinplate, most of which originated in South Wales. In that year, however, the imposition of the McKinley Tariff enabled the Americans to give protection to their own emerging tinplate industry, and caused a prolonged slump in Wales. Whereas in 1891 some 25,000 people were employed in tinplate manufacture, by 1898 the number had dropped to 16,000. Between 1895 and 1899 no less than 36 tinplate businesses had to halt production, and some including nearby Carmarthen - simply closed down. The slump caused thousands of Welsh tinplate workers to emigrate to the United States, where they helped to build up the industry in the USA. 'Sooner or later', McKinley very shrewdly observed 'the Welsh tinplate industry will come to us'.

By 1892 the Kidwelly Tinplate works was feeling the ill effects of this depression, and it had become common for the 700 employees to experience protracted lay-offs. In June all work ceased, and it was announced that the works would remain closed for the rest of the year. As the works were now by far the largest employers in the district, this was a serious matter, and even before the autumn there was considerable poverty and distress in the town. The Mayor of Kidwelly, Captain Daniel Harries, felt unable to get involved by organising relief because he was also the manager of the tinplate works. In November 1892, however, a new mayor was elected, namely Alderman Daniel Stephens. As many families were now in a desperate plight, he abandoned the usual mayoral banquet in order to give the money to the poor. A few weeks later, in December, it was announced that Captain Harries had resigned as works manager, and would be moving to take up a post at the Glanamman works.

Early in 1893 the Kidwelly Tinplate works resumed production under the management of David Griffiths, formerly of the Ashburnham works at Pembrey. Only six mills out of a possible 11 were brought into use, but even on this restricted production the business was struggling to cope in a deeply depressed trade. In September the employees were laid off until November, renewing what was becoming a pattern of intermittent and erratic periods of work. Unfortunately, at the same period there were difficulties also in the silica brick business. The full story is far from clear, but John Coley Bromford, who had become Chairman of the Kidwelly R. Dinas Fire Brick Co. in 1889, was reported in January 1893 to have been made bankrupt. George Redford, who had come back into the business with a substantial shareholding, was appointed liquidator in March 1893, and by November he had completed the company's winding up. Although documentary evidence has yet to come to light, it is thought that within a year or two the brickworks site and business had been taken over by Henry Smart.

Inevitably all these events had some impact on the traffic of the GVR, and business was not helped by the closure of limekilns at Mynydd-y-Garreg in 1894. It is possible that Threlfall's kilns of 1872 were closed for some time, but the main casualty appears to have been the slightly older group of kilns attributed to Owen Bowen. What is certain is that the Mynydd-y-Garreg & Kidwelly Railway & Lime Co. was wound up in 1894, but somehow the Gwendraeth Valleys Railway managed not to be brought down with it. As the uncomfortable 1890s continued the only solace the Directors could offer themselves and the shareholders was the repeated assertion that the railway was in good order. The report for the half-year to 30th June, 1895, noted that the tin works had been standing idle for most of that period 'and in consequence the amount of traffic has been small'. Indeed it seems the works was in production for a mere 14 weeks in the whole of 1895, so it was quite natural at the end of the year for the Directors to lament the 'continuing dullness in the tinplate trade'. In the meantime they had also had good reason to lament the death of their Chairman, William Slater. True to form, in the Manchester era, Mr Slater's son, Robert Leighton Slater, was appointed to the Board. In the following year George T. Hardman resigned from Board, and was replaced by James Henry Hardman.

Unfortunately matters now went from bad to worse. In April 1896 the *Llanelly Mercury* noted that the works had been closed since the New Year, and reported that 'there are dozens of cases where hunger rules the home and heads of families do not know where to turn to feed their young children'. The workmen were said to be ready to accept wages 7½ per cent lower than those received by tinplate workers in Llanelli. The management was seeking an overall reduction in wages of about 22½ per cent! No real progress was made in resolving these differences, and in October 1896 it was announced that all staff had been discharged. The then manager, James E. Paton, was granted the dubious consolation of being appointed works caretaker.

Inevitably the shut down of the tinplate works had a depressing effect upon the GVR. At the end of 1896 traffic was described by the Receiver as 'again . . . very poor', although at the end of 1897 he was able to say that 'a large amount has been spent upon the line this half year, the worst portion having been relaid'. He added that 'a considerable amount has been received from the sale of the old material. The line is presently in good order.' Plainly such sales were essential for any kind of maintenance to continue. In the second half of 1898 the receipts were barely a quarter of those earned in the second half of 1890! By 1898, however, the Receiver had had enough, and was ready to sell the GVR if a buyer could be found. The most obvious potential purchaser was the BP&GV, although this company also had its financial problems. As will be seen from Appendix Two in June 1898 George Williamson made contact with the BP&GV with this in mind, but received a very cautious response. The one feature of the GVR which was clearly attractive to the larger company was the link between Tycoch and the South Wales main line. Unfortunately this was the one piece of line which had not been provided for in any of the early Acts of Parliament, and so was of uncertain legal status. In the event a sale did not take place.

After a long period of difficulty and inactivity, the Tinplate works were put up for sale again in April 1899. In July it was learned that the purchasers were a syndicate led by John Thomas of Llangennech. They promptly formed a new company entitled the Kidwelly Iron Sheet and Tinplate Company (KIS&TP) with an authorised capital of £40,000 in £500 shares. The works had been acquired for just £14,000, and it must be assumed that the balance was intended for new investment, although in fact not all the shares were taken up. At all events, the new company was seen as the salvation of Kidwelly, and at once the streets were made colourful with bunting. Amid general rejoicing the works were partially re-opened in July, with John Thomas as Managing Director. By November 1899 full production had resumed, and at the end of the year George Williamson, the GVR's Secretary, noted that the 'Tin works have now been going for about six months, and better results are looked for'.

This hope seemed to be fulfilled in the half-yearly report at the end of June 1900, when the Directors of the railway were 'happy to call attention to the improvement in results . . .' Unfortunately, by the end of the year the familiar 'stop-start' pattern of operation had re-asserted itself, and the Directors stated gloomily, 'the Tin Works have again stopped working, and consequently the Revenue Account for the half year shows badly. It is quite uncertain when this state of affairs may be improved'. The GVR Board was not able to offer the debenture holders any encouragement either: '. . . in consequence of a heavier locomotive now being used, and by reason of a bridge on the line requiring renewal, a fairly large expenditure is now required . . . for this reason it is necessary to keep cash in hand instead of paying anything against debenture interest'.

In the following months the bridge and track repairs were carried out, but as the tinplate works remained idle the railway's income got no better. Why the works remained closed is uncertain, but it implies either serious technical deficiencies or, more likely, poor management and inept marketing. At this period the Boer War was at its height, and tinplate was needed for ammunition boxes, tinned provisions and other purposes. Somehow this demand was not matched by action at Kidwelly. Indeed, by 1902 the proprietors were looking for a way out. The works was put up for auction, although withdrawn with the bidding at £8,000. In June 1902 the KIS&TP Co. entered into an agreement to sell its plant and equipment for salvage or scrap to one of the shareholders, David Evans of Llangennech Park; in October 1902, however, the freehold in the site seems to have been conveyed to members of the Thomas family. At the time neither of these moves appeared to bode well for the works, and according to a GVR report in 1903 'the works are in fact gradually getting broken up'. The KIS&TP Co. resolved to go into voluntary liquidation in April 1903, but only the older Lower Works were actually dismantled. The much younger and more extensive Upper Works site now became the focus of attention for an engineer and iron producer named Charles E. Peel. In January 1904 he agreed to take a lease of the tinplate works, and in July 1904, with David Evans and others, he formed a new company called simply the Kidwelly Tinplate Company. Initially this had an authorised capital of £40,000 in £10 shares; later the authorised capital was increased to £60,000. Without any doubt, this new team hoped to break out of the depressing cycle of mismanagement or misfortune which had afflicted the business, and one of the earliest results was their decision to negotiate for the purchase of the Gwendraeth Valleys Railway.

In doing so, it would seem they managed to deflect fresh consideration of a possible sale of the GVR to the BP&GVR. Even so, interest in the idea was sufficiently strong for a draft deed for such a transaction to be prepared.

The Directors' half-yearly report for the period to 30th June, 1904, stated that 'an agreement has been come to for the sale of the railway to parties representing the Tinplate Co., and this will be carried out in the next two or three months'. Serious difficulties must have been encountered, because within a very short time there was also discussion about the possible abandonment of the railway. Indeed, in August 1904, the required minimum 5 per cent of shareholders lodged a petition in favour of abandonment. On 13th September, 1904, these shareholders (who included Mrs M.A. Threlfall and George Williamson) called an extraordinary general meeting of the GVR under the Abandonment of Railways Act, 1850, on the grounds that the Directors of the company had 'failed for 14 days after the receipt of a requisition . . . under the provisions of the Act to convene a meeting for the purpose'. The fact of the matter was that most of the Manchester shareholders had had enough, and certainly had no desire to throw good money after bad. A clear majority, said to represent £99,500 of capital, approved the proposal to abandon the line.

This decision was not at all welcome in Kidwelly. For all its financial frailty, the GVR was a necessary transport facility for local industry, and the Borough of Kidwelly itself owned limestone and silica quarries at Mynydd-y-Garreg. Urgent efforts were made to resolve the issue, and in due course it was agreed that shares in the GVR should be transferred to nominees of local interests, most notably the Kidwelly Tinplate Company. Accordingly the Tinplate company acquired the whole of the share and loan stock of the GVR for just £3,000. The new proprietors did not suppose that the railway could be worked for a profit, but they could see that it was essential for the works to have adequate railway facilities for it to have any future prospects. Early in December 1904, John Henry Hall and James Henry Hardman resigned as Directors of the railway, and it appears that at the same period their colleague Robert Leighton Slater also stepped down. These men represented the Manchester interest in the Kidwelly district, and during their reign Board meetings had almost invariably taken place at the company's offices at 37 Brown Street, Manchester. The new Board comprised men with deep roots in South Wales, and their meetings usually took place at the Hotel Metropole in Swansea. Such was the case on 28th March, 1905, when Colonel J.R. Wright took the chair, the other new Directors present being Major Wright, John Thomas, C.E. Peel, and W. Gilson Morris. The resignation of George Williamson was promptly accepted, and instead Mr Henry Smart was appointed Manager and Secretary at the very modest salary of £50 per annum.

Chapter Six

The Kidwelly Tinplate Period, 1905-1923

In Colonel John Roper Wright the new Board of the GVR had gained the expertise and influence of a notable and well-respected South Wales industrialist. Born in Lancashire in 1843, he moved to Swansea in 1874 to work with William Siemens at his Landore Iron & Steel works. In 1878 he was one of three partners who bought and re-opened the Elba Steelworks at Gowerton, and in the same year produced the first open-hearth steel ingot to be manufactured into tinplate. The firm prospered as the first specialist producers of steel suitable for manufacturing tinplate, and in 1882 it acquired the Panteg Steelworks, and in 1889 the Cwmavon Iron Works, although this was closed two years later. In 1887 the company became known as Wright, Butler & Co., and continued to expand under Col Wright's chairmanship, re-opening the Pontymoile Tinworks in 1892, and acquiring the Landore Iron & Steel Co. in 1900. By the turn of the century Wright, Butler & Co. was working closely with another well known steel manufacturer, Messrs Baldwins, and in 1902 the two firms were merged. At the same period Col Wright held directorships in a number of colliery companies, one of which was Whitworth Collieries Ltd, proprietors of a mine at Tonmawr, east of Neath. In the Act of Parliament authorising the construction of the Port Talbot Railway & Dock Co. in 1894, Col Wright was named as one of the provisional Directors. He was soon elected Deputy Chairman, and became Chairman on 19th June, 1908, in place of Lord Dunraven. Meanwhile, as a result of a working agreement made in 1907 between the Port Talbot Railway and the neighbouring South Wales Mineral Railway, he became Chairman of the latter concern in February 1908. Accordingly, by the summer of that year, Col Wright achieved the unique distinction of being Chairman simultaneously of three South Wales railway companies.

In keeping with Col Wright's activities, the other new Directors of the GVR were also men of diverse talents and interests. Charles Wright, his son, made a flying start by being appointed a Director of Messrs Baldwins in 1902, when aged 26, and for a time he was manager of the Elba steelworks at Gowerton. Charles E. Peel was part owner of the Trimsaran Iron & Steel Co. in 1902. He also became a Director of the Gyrnos Tinplate Works. John Paton, thought to be the son of David Paton (mentioned in the previous chapter) was a rope manufacturer in Llanelly. Together these men set about improving the Upper Works at Kidwelly. By 1908 seven mills were in use, and no less than 350 people were employed, although an inquiry into working conditions in 1911 was distinctly critical. Evidently in many areas of the works the labour was arduous, and the dust and fumes potentially hazardous to health - most notably in the tin house. Put another way, if a health and safety inspector of the 1990s had visited the works at that time he would surely have wished to shut it all down!

Under the new dispensation the GVR became a wholly owned subsidiary of

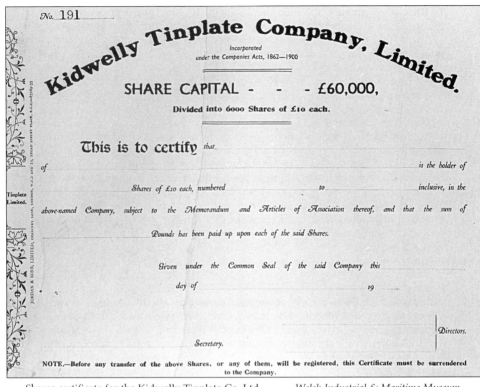

№ 191

Kidwelly Tinplate Company, Limited.

Incorporated
under the Companies Acts, 1862—1900

SHARE CAPITAL - - - £60,000,

Divided into 6000 Shares of £10 each.

This is to certify _that_____

_of_ _____ _is the holder of_

_____ _Shares of £10 each, numbered_ _____ _to_ _____ _inclusive, in the_

above-named Company, subject to the Memorandum and Articles of Association thereof, and that the sum of

_____ _Pounds has been paid up upon each of the said Shares._

Given under the Common Seal of the said Company this _____

day of _____ 19_____

_____
Directors.

Secretary.

NOTE.—Before any transfer of the above Shares, or any of them, will be registered, this Certificate must be surrendered to the Company.

Shares certificate for the Kidwelly Tinplate Co. Ltd.   _Welsh Industrial & Maritime Museum_

Below, left: W.J. Francis, the GVR's accountant and, _right_: H.E. Smart Manager and Secretary.
GWR Magazine

the Kidwelly Tinplate Co., although initially the finances of the parent company appear to have been in an even more parlous condition than those of the Gwendraeth Valleys. In 1906 it was decided that the Tinplate Co.'s private owner wagons and covered vans should be transferred to the GVR at the price at which they stood in the Tinplate Co.'s books on 30th June, 1906 - £606 13s. 4d. This was done with effect from 1st July, and in the words of a minute of 12th September, it was agreed to 'arrange with the Bank to increase the Railway overdraft by £300 and reduce the Tinplate Co.'s overdraft by the amount of the cheque received from the G.V. Rly Co'.

The new management undoubtedly strengthened the GVR financially, their first step being the purchase of a new steam locomotive. In view of Col Wright's knowledge of railway company business, it is thought that he may have made a personal contribution to the acquisition. At all events the locomotive was ordered in December 1904, from Hudswell, Clarke & Co. of Leeds, and was delivered in 1905, being named originally *Kidwelly*, and later *Velindre*. Next the Directors embarked on a policy of track renewal, which eventually saw most of the line relaid with steel rails weighing 75 1b./yard bolted directly onto the sleepers. By 1908 thought was being given to the possibility of acquiring another engine. In March of that year a decision to purchase was deferred, but on 8th June, 1909 Col Wright declared that 'he would see what he could do in the way of purchasing a second-hand locomotive from the GWR Co'. Even so, another nine months elapsed before it was decided, on 3rd March, 1910, that Lt Col C.W. Wright and H.E. Smart, the company Secretary, should approach the GWR 'with a view to purchasing a second locomotive from that company'. Eventually, in June, the Directors agreed to purchase GWR No. 1378, *Margaret*, for the sum of £800, delivered to Kidwelly. Certain repairs and improvements had to be affected, and it was not until January 1911 that the engine began work.

Quite naturally, the Directors had a concern for good housekeeping, and at their meeting on 3rd March, 1910 they decided they could offer a plot of land at the rear of the locomotive shed for sale for £200. They also discussed certain rebate allowances granted by the GWR, but decided not to pursue the matter at that moment. The issue dated back to 1877, when a GVR desperate for survival had negotiated an allowance from the Great Western of 1d. or 2d. per ton (depending on the type of goods) on all freight transferred between the two companies. In 1908 the GWR had proposed to abolish the rebate, but were dissuaded by an urgent appeal from the GVR. The threat remained, however, and the Directors tried to use their wits to defer the decision as long as possible.

The close association between the GVR and the Tinplate Co. appears to have become increasingly intimate, to the extent that in February 1913 it was decided that in future GVR Board meetings would only be required annually. As the two companies had a largely similar directorate, and the manager of the tinplate works, John Thomas, was on the Board of the GVR, there was no doubt about the daily operations of the railway being mainly for the benefit of traffic to and from the tinplate works. Even so, as will be seen in the next chapter, the limestone, silica sand and brick industries still wished to be served by the railway. The scale of Col Wright's industrial interest across South Wales, as

Kidwelly Tinplate Works *c.* 1930. *Author's Collection*

An aerial view of Kidwelly Tinplate works from the south-east showing the proximity of the river, rail links and the rural setting for such a large works. *Roger Worsley*

well as the fact of the close link between the companies, may have had a bearing on a change of outlook towards the GVR. In the 19th century the GWR, in particular, had been willing to accept the GVR as a railway company in its own right, but now with a major industrialist in charge, it began to see the whole line as little more than a siding to the Kidwelly tinplate works. Arguably this attitude became most apparent in 1911, when the Great Western required the GVR's motive power to be registered (like those of other industrial concerns) for running over GWR tracks.

Improvements to the GVR prior to World War I were matched by a steady rather than spectacular growth in traffic. Even in 1912, when there was a notable strike in the nearby and vitally important coal industry, the Gwendraeth Valleys line managed to keep going relatively successfully, with receipts higher than in 1910. The peak year for traffic weights (rather than receipts) was 1913, when over 123,000 tons passed over the line. Of this, 54,378 tons originated on the GVR. Stone constituted by far the largest tonnage carried, at 24,443 tons, whilst tinplate provided 13,761 tons. Some of 8,688 tons of bricks were conveyed away, but the figures for other commodities like iron and sand were quite small. Most years expenditure matched income, or exceeded it, providing no net revenue at all - but in 1913 the GVR recorded a profit of £583.

Although the onset of World War I was a general stimulus to the national economy, this was not reflected in much greater traffic on the little Gwendraeth Valleys Railway. Indeed, the fact that the GVR frequently produced negligible or negative figures for net revenue made the Directors very mindful of other elements in the balance sheet. Their concern continued over the GWR's rebate on freight rates, and although one source suggests that the rebates ended in 1914, other evidence indicates that it lasted until 1916. Certainly on 23rd December, 1915, the Directors found it necessary to discuss raising their own rates to customers, and it was agreed that from 1st January, 1916, a basic rate of 6*d.*/ton would be charged. On 28th March, 1916, this decision was confirmed, with the clarification that it would be levied on all traffic in and out of the works of the Kidwelly Tinplate Co., and 'for services rendered in marshalling and shunting their traffic'.

From time to time the minutes of the GVR make mention of more personal matters. The company's accountant W.J. Francis was plainly in favour, because in March 1910 he was awarded a salary increase of 5s. per week, and in January 1913 an increase of 10s. per week! H.E. Smart, the company Secretary, had his salary increased to £200 per annum in February 1914, whilst much later, in 1919, he was the recipient of a 50 guinea honorarium. The most notable change, though, came in 1915 with the departure of no less than four GVR Directors, Col J.R. Wright, his son, now Col C.W. Wright, John Paton and W.G. Morris. The reasons for the resignation of the last two are not known. The Wrights, however, were going on to greater things.

By this time Col J.R. Wright was a Director of the Port Talbot Steel Co. Ltd, and now in 1915 took up the important post of Controller of Iron and Steel Production for the Ministry of Munitions, serving in this capacity until his health deteriorated in 1917. He was succeeded by his son, who continued in

Sir John Roper Wright, Chairman of the Gwendraeth Valleys Railway, 1904-1915.
Welsh Industrial & Maritime Museum

office until in 1919. In 1920 both father and son had the unusual distinction of receiving knighthoods in the same year. Sir John Wright died in 1926, whilst Sir Charles Wright went on to gather other notable directorships, and to be President of the British Iron & Steel Federation in 1937-38. In 1940 he became Controller of Iron & Steel Production in the Ministry of Supply, and served until 1943 when his health failed. He died in 1950.

Given these commitments it is not entirely surprising that the Wrights left the Board of the GVR! However, their replacements were also very capable men. Daniel Williams and Herbert Eccles were both Directors of the Llanelly Steel Co., the latter being Managing Director. Williams was also a Director of two nearby tinplate works, the Old Castle at Llanelly and the Ashburnham at Burry Port, whilst Eccles was Chairman of the Briton Ferry steelworks, and of the South Wales Siemens Steel Association. In addition he had a variety of interests in the tinplate industry, and was actually the proprietor of the Resolven Tinplate Works in the Vale of Neath.

Wartime conditions favoured most heavy industries, but certain restrictions were placed on the production of tinplate which did not help the Kidwelly works. By 1918 the quantity of tinplate carried on the GVR was less than half that conveyed in 1913. On the other hand, Alexander Young's brickworks near Graig were extended in 1917, and the tonnage of bricks passing over the railway was the highest recorded at 9,686 tons. Limestone traffic was also at a high level that year, with 31,382 tons transported over the GVR. In complete contrast, though, the tonnage of sand conveyed dropped from 2,593 in 1913 to a mere 64 tons in 1918.

Early in the war British railway companies were taken under government control for the duration of hostilities, but rather surprisingly there is no reference to this situation in the few GVR minutes available for the period. In 1919 many railway companies were facing difficulties with increased operating costs, and to give time to debate future policy it was decided to maintain government control of the railways for a further two years. Unfortunately the GVR's status in this process is not entirely clear; although government control would be expected for a public railway company, a minute dated 30th September, 1919 suggests that the GVR may have been omitted from the original scheme, presumably as an industrial undertaking. According to the minute, the Board asked the company Secretary to see the solicitors and the auditor 'to learn what steps if any should be taken to place the company under government control'.

Whatever the facts on this point, the GVR did come under the terms of the Railways Act, 1921, which sought to gather 123 railway companies into four substantial groupings. It was decreed that the smaller companies in South Wales should be incorporated into an enlarged Great Western Railway, and some were absorbed in this way in 1922. From the viewpoint of the GWR, the Gwendraeth Valleys line must have seemed a marginal case, and they did not view it with any great sense of excitement. However, officers of the GWR, were sent to Kidwelly to make inspections of the railway, and the reports printed in Appendix Three reveal a good deal about the state of the line at this time.

In July 1922, E. Lowther of the Chief Goods Manager's Office at Paddington gave quite an encouraging account of the GVR's traffic. Perhaps his most interesting comment was the suggestion that the West Wales coal traffic could be diverted to the Kidwelly route - implying much heavier use of the connection with the BP&GV line at Tycoch. The report also refers to an earlier report, touching on staff economies. Unfortunately up to date figures for staff and wages were not then available, and those given related to the first week of December 1912! At that time three men were engaged in permanent way work at a total cost of £2 15s. 8d. for the week. Another three men were employed on operating and traffic duties at a cost of £4 10s. 11d. per week, and there were two guards with wages totalling £2 19s. 2d. One man - surely a part-timer - was employed as a signalman and gateman for just 2s. per week. In addition to these nine employees, there were no less than three salaried staff - H.E. Smart, the Manager and company Secretary, W.J. Francis, the accountant, and also a clerk. Together these three were paid £5 2s. 4d. for the week. This was not a state of affairs much liked by the GWR. Looking to the future, in 1922 it was declared that the 'Manager, Accountant and Junior Clerk could be dispensed with . . . There is no doubt, however, that any possible economies would be swallowed up for some years by the cost of putting the permanent way in order'.

By the time the shareholders held their AGM at the Hotel Metropole on 10th October, 1922, the negotiations with the GWR were the main item of business. After hearing the correspondence, it was agree that John Thomas, Henry Smart, and the company solicitor should attend a meeting at Paddington to continue discussions. Although the terms offered to GVR shareholders were less generous than they would have wished, their representatives were not in a strong position to argue. To reach a settlement the Great Western proposed the issue of £33,300 worth of GWR 2½ per cent debenture stock in exchange for the GVR's debenture loans, the ordinary shares of the GVR being cancelled, with the company to be handed over freed from all liability with regard to unpaid interest. The last GVR shareholders' meeting was duly held at the Hotel Metropole on 12th December, with Daniel Williams in the chair. He put forward the proposal that the preliminary absorption scheme be approved 'subject to such modifications as may be determined by the Directors and approved by the Railways Amalgamation Tribunal, or as may be made by that Tribunal'. The resolution was carried unanimously, and the Gwendraeth Valleys Railway became part of the Great Western Railway with effect from 1st January, 1923. It was the smallest of all the railway companies affected by the 1921 Railways Act, and thus the smallest to be absorbed by the GWR.

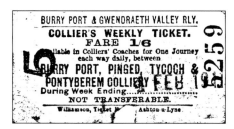

Courtesy T. David

Chapter Seven

The Kidwelly Silica Wars and After

The year 1901 saw the climax of a complex dispute between the Kidwelly Corporation, which owned virtually all the limestone and silica on Mynydd-y-Garreg, and certain producers, most notably Stephens & Co. The drama was intensified by the fact that most ratepayers supported Messrs Stephens rather than the Corporation, whilst a majority of the elected councillors were sympathetic to the interests of Alexander Young. Such was the ferocity of the argument in 1901 that the local press was moved to describe the row as 'the Kidwelly silica wars'.

As with many disputes, the 'silica wars' had a lengthy history. As early as 1840 it seems that the Corporation granted a lease of minerals on Mynydd-y-Garreg to a Mr Webb for a rent of £5 per annum. 'Minerals', in this context, appear to have been non-ferrous metals, and although there was some working of low-grade copper ore near Graig Farm in the mid-Victorian period the operation is not thought to have been very productive. In the ensuing years there were numerous minor lettings of stone for building or for limestone burning in the several small limekilns dotted about on Mynydd-y-Garreg. In 1861, as has been noted, Kidwelly Corporation agreed to grant Owen Bowen the right to work limestone adjoining his proposed branch railway, and for a few years at least Bowen operated his own kilns. In 1881 the Corporation leased a portion of Mynydd-y-Garreg to Henry Smart for 50 years backdated to run from 29th September, 1876, at a dead rent of £25 per annum. In addition the lessee had to pay a royalty of 5d./ton for silica sand and 3d./ton for silica stone, and was also subject to a penalty of £5/ton for every ton removed without prior weighing. In 1895 a lease of another part of Mynydd-y-Garreg was granted on very similar terms to Daniel Stephens. In this case the 50-year lease was backdated to 25th March, 1893, and Stephens also covenanted not to cart stone or sand other than to the Wern Terrace siding (later known as Minkie Road, or simply 'the Sidings') on the Gwendraeth Valleys Railway.

For a while, all was well. In a letter to the *Llanelly & County Guardian* in July 1900, a number of Kidwelly councillors described the course of events:

As a matter of practice Mr Smart has carted all the sand and stone from his quarry to the said siding and taken it from thence over the Gwendraeth Valley Railway to his works, and Mr Daniel Stephens has carted the bulk of the stone worked from his said quarry to the same siding and taken them thence by the same railway to the terminus adjacent to his works. None of the stone has ever been weighed before its removal from the quarries, but the Council have from time to time been informed that it was weighed on the said railway. The Council have for some time been dissatisfied with the returns of the quantities of stone and sand worked, and became aware that stone was supplied from Stephens' quarry for the repair of the roads in adjoining parishes, for which the Council received no return and consequently received no royalty for it. When this was mentioned in the Council, of which Mr Stephens is a member, he admitted it and said the Council should look after their own business, and the Council was likewise informed that the hauliers occasionally took loads of stone from the quarry direct to the works, and which consequently was not weighed on the railroad.

In the light of these developments Kidwelly Corporation understandably decided that they needed a weighbridge of their own. Both Smart and Stephens seem to have ignored the suggestion that they might contribute to the cost, and showed a marked reluctance to have anything to do with it. Furthermore a proposed charge for the use of the weighbridge was seen as an obstacle to its operation. When Stephens declared that his business had been 'harassed' by the Corporation, councillors retorted that,

> . . . the Council declined to give them a practical monopoly of the silica material on the Corporation lands upon Messrs Stephens own terms. So far from 'harassing' them , the Council having ascertained that 40 tons of stone had been removed from the quarries for repairing the roads in neighbouring parishes, in respect of which Messrs Stephens had made no return and paid no royalty, the Council instead of charging the penal royalty of £/ton . . . have let them off with paying 3d./ton only.

Just to add to the recriminations, at the same time the Corporation was involved in a separate dispute with Mr Smart over the provision of stone for the repair of roads within Kidwelly parish.

These arguments were part of the background to the larger dispute which now ensued. In January 1899 the Corporation had discussed an application from Messrs Stephens for the lease of a further 3¾ acres of Mynydd-y-Garreg, and in response had proposed an amalgamation of the old and new leases, charging a dead rent of £100 per annum, and a royalty of 6d./ton. These terms being more onerous than those applied previously, they were declared unacceptable, and it seems that for a time the Stephens' quarry was closed. Barely two years later, though, the Corporation entered into negotiation with William Young (believed to be the son of Alexander Young) regarding a lease of over 280 acres, or most of Mynydd-y-Garreg, for a dead rent of just £30 per annum. Not only were these terms preferential, but as the Youngs already had rights to stone in a sizeable tract of the Brigstocke estate at Four Roads, the entire proposal must have seemed insulting to Messrs Stephens. They were outraged, and the anger was shared by many ratepayers. As councillors, Daniel and Alfred Stephens were well placed to voice their opinions, but the scheme had significant backing from other members, who included both William Young and his solicitor, Mr Browne. The *Llanelly & County Guardian* expressed the popular view in a leading article published on 9th May, 1901:

> Whatever may be the relations between Mr Browne, Messrs Stephens and Mr Young, the Corporation has a clear duty to perform, and that is to farm out public estate without fear or favour, to the best possible advantage. No one can contend that by leasing the whole of the unlet portion of the mountain for a wretched £30 a year, the Corporation have made a good bargain for their constituents. What wonder, then, that the ratepayers should seek to show in some not-to-be-mistaken manner, that they disapprove of what their representatives have done. There seems, also, to be an indecent haste in endeavouring to get the lease drafted. To us this is a very disquieting feature of the whole proceedings.

The newspaper did not exaggerate the hostility of the ratepayers. The fact that neither Stephens nor Smart had been straightforward in their previous dealings with the Corporation paled into insignificance. The ratepayers believed that this deal was wrong, and the verbatim press reports of several meetings were coloured by rancour and recriminations. Early in May 1901, a meeting of the Kidwelly Corporation was marked by scenes more appropriate to a football match. 'Uproar' was one description; 'daylight robbery' the opinion of a ratepayer; the 'Kidwelly silica wars' was the verdict of the press. This monumental row reached its climax two months later when at another stormy meeting of the Corporation a majority of councillors decided to seal the lease in favour of Councillor Young. The *Llanelly & County Guardian* was again severely critical of the Corporation, implying that some members had been motivated more by personal animosity 'than by regard for the public weal'.

If the dispute was well publicised, the aftermath was less so. In July 1901 it was suggested that an injunction might be obtained to prevent the Corporation from granting the lease on such controversial terms. It is not yet clear whether the objectors made any progress by resorting to law. What is apparent is that within a very few years there was a shift in power and influence in Kidwelly in favour of Messrs Stephens. This may have been the electoral consequence of pursuing such a profoundly unpopular measure; it may have had some connection with Alexander Young's death, which is thought to have occurred between 1903 and 1905. At all events, the Youngs appear to have made relatively little use of their rights on Mynydd-y-Garreg beyond the opening of a clay and silica quarry near Graig Farm. Before World War I, however, Messrs Stephens had negotiated access to a large area at the southern end of Mynydd-y-Garreg and were poised for a further expansion of their business. Given the very different history of Young's and Stephens, the two concerns will now be considered separately.

Alexander Young, Four Roads

In 1822 William Weston Young invented a means of manufacturing firebricks using silica and some added lime. He built a brickworks at Dinas, north of Glyn Neath, where silica rock had been worked for a generation. His refractory bricks for lining furnaces proved to be a great success, and became famous in many parts of the world. Indeed, it is said that in both German and Russian the word 'dinas' was adopted as a term for 'firebrick'. In the United Kingdom the word 'dinas' was certainly regarded as an indication of quality, and was frequently incorporated into the titles of brick-producing companies.

The Young family is believed to have been extensive, and relatives of William Weston Young were involved in several areas of firebrick manufacture. Alexander Young may not have been a direct descendant of W.W. Young, but undoubtedly he shared his interest in silica, limestone and the firebrick industry. As has been noted, in 1877 he erected a bank of five limekilns at Penymynydd Farm, Four Roads. Built of dressed stone, these kilns stood adjacent to Young's own standard gauge railway which ran down to a junction with the GVR at Mynydd-y-Garreg. According to one local story Alexander Young had an arrangement with five local farmers whereby each was allocated

Young's Brickworks, north of Mynydd-y-Garreg. The metal bar resting on this section of brickwork is part of the old name stamp used in the brickyard. The inverted letters read 'A.Y.Dinas', 29th February, 1996.   *Author*

Young's Brickworks, north of Mynydd-y-Garreg. Brick kilns stood on the extreme right, and the two brick structures in the centre supported a gas engine. The car in the gateway stands on the line of the old railway, which followed the track towards the camera. The slightly raised ground between the camera and the brickworks marks the site of a loading platform for rail traffic, 29th February, 1996.   *Author*

the use of one of the kilns. Hitherto local agricultural requirements had been met by the production of lime at the small and isolated farmers' kilns to be found at a number of sites around Mynydd-y-Garreg. If the local story is correct the use of Young's kilns would probably have been more efficient and convenient, although it is also clear from the scale of Young's investment and activity that the kilns were set up as a fully commercial venture, and not merely for the benefit of a few farmers.

It is thought that Young's railway was constructed at the time the limekilns were built; it is depicted on an edition of the Ordnance Survey prepared in 1879. After making use of about 800 yards of the abandoned C&CR earthworks, the remaining 1,300 yards were laid on a steadily rising gradient across the fields to Penymynydd Farm. About 150 yards from the end of the line a loop and siding was provided adjacent to the limekilns. There was also a small weigh-house and office, and in the early years there is believed to have been a timber trestle carrying a stone loading shoot from the top of the kilns to the siding. The track then took to a ferocious gradient - perhaps as steep as 1 in 15 - to terminate at a small stone-built locomotive shed next to Penymynydd Farm. Adjoining the railway on this short section was situated 'Stabl Young', and a stone building known as 'Ty Sand', the 'Sand House'. The primary purpose of the latter appears to have been to provide a store for equipment and spares, although its name probably derived from the existence of a furnace to dry sand. The stable is said to have been provided for the horse mainly used to move drams or wagons in the quarry situated behind the kilns. A short and steeply graded siding ran from the engine shed up towards the quarry, terminating near the top of the kilns.

According to a note in BP&GVR papers, a locomotive belonging to Young was repaired at Burry Port in 1887. Sadly no further information about it has come to light. However, on 19th March, 1902, the *Western Mail* carried the following advert:

LOCOMOTIVE wanted; about 13 inches cylinders; 6 wheels coupled; wheels low - state age, builder's name, and full particulars and lowest price to A. Young, Kidwelly, South Wales.

The appeal was evidently successful, because just over three years later another advert appeared regarding the engine's disposal:

LOCOMOTIVE, saddle tank, six wheels coupled, 12 inch cylinders, For sale at very low price, left off working at 120 1b. pressure - apply A. Young, Kidwelly.

Unfortunately again there is a teasing lack of additional information.

According to the records of the Industrial Railway Society an 0-4-0ST named *Duxbury* was at work on the line by 1908. This engine had been built by Hudswell, Clarke of Leeds in 1882 (Works No. 238) and for many years gave service at the Duxbury Park colliery, Bolton. Somewhat surprisingly there is no local memory of an engine of this name, although quite a number of elderly residents clearly recall a locomotive painted black and named *Dyvatty*. The only known engine of this name was the Peckett 0-6-0ST (Works No. 498 of

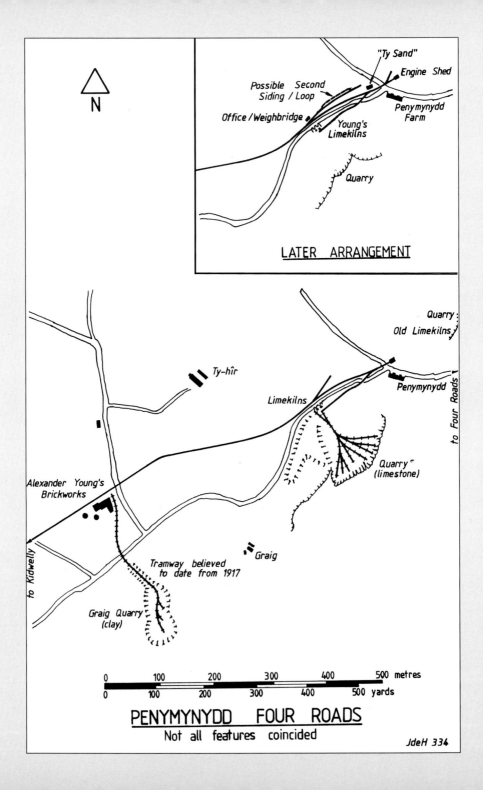

N

"Ty Sand"
Engine Shed
Possible Second
Siding / Loop
Penymynydd
Farm
Office/Weighbridge
Young's
Limekilns
Quarry

LATER ARRANGEMENT

Quarry
Old Limekilns
Ty-hîr
Penymynydd
Limekilns
to Four Roads
Quarry
(limestone)
Alexander Young's
Brickworks
Graig
to Kidwelly
Tramway believed
to date from 1917
Graig Quarry
(clay)

| 0 | 100 | 200 | 300 | 400 | 500 metres |
| 0 | 100 | 200 | 300 | 400 | 500 yards |

PENYMYNYDD FOUR ROADS
Not all features coincided

JdeH 334

1891) which ran on the neighbouring BP&GVR until 1906. The available details of the later career of *Dyvatty* make no mention of a period at Four Roads, which may permit some speculation over the possibility of the engine's nameplates being transferred to a locomotive operated on Alexander Young's line. Some of the memories of Young's *Dyvatty* point to it being a four-coupled saddle tank, although there is a degree of doubt.

By the end of the 19th century Young had decided to expand his business interests by building his own silica brickworks on land at Highgate, near Graig, north of Mynydd-y-Garreg. The foundations for the brickworks were laid by Mrs Young in August 1900. According to a press report dated 18th August, 1900, Alexander Young was the proprietor of the 'Graig and Mynydd Uchaf Lime Works and Silica Sand Pits'. In his speech Young said that whilst it was over 23 years since the foundation of the stone lime kilns, there was no better place in the Principality for the erection of a silica brick works, because 'here before us we have a mountain of silica rock of the best quality, also large deposits of silica sand and clay, and with a railway and all the material on the premises it looks good for the future'.

Unfortunately this development soon became controversial. As has been described, Kidwelly Corporation's readiness to grant Messrs Young a lease on very favourable terms sparked the 'silica wars'. By now William Young appears to have been the most active figure in the business, and Alexander was becoming elderly. Indeed, Alexander did not have much longer to enjoy his achievements. Although, in February 1903, he signed an agreement with the BP&GVR in respect of certain premises at Kidwelly, he is thought to have died soon afterwards. According to the Kidwelly historian, Revd D. Daven Jones, writing in 1907, Young was then deceased and the limekilns at Penymynydd were out of use. At this period Mrs Young and William Young were resident at Glanmorfa, Station Road, Kidwelly. The business continued, however, trading after 1908 as 'A.Y. Dinas Silica Brick & Lime Co.', most of the firm's output being the refractory brick used in the iron and steel industry. Aided no doubt by the onset of World War I, the company enjoyed some success, and by 1917 plans were in hand to enlarge the works.

In its original form the brickworks is believed to have had four kilns. The expansion provided for the construction of two more kilns and another chimney stack, two crushers, a drying stove, panmills, a brick press, and a number of smaller items. It was also intended to remove an old steam engine, and to make some alterations to roofs to accommodate the new plant. Although no documentary evidence has come to light on the point, one interesting innovation is said to have been made at this time, namely the installation of a gas engine. It is recorded, perhaps surprisingly, that the extensions required the purchase of substantial quantities of bricks from other brickworks - most notably 108,750 Trimsaran building bricks, and 23,668 Hancocks firebricks. Some metal fittings were manufactured at the Burry Port Foundry. The total cost of these works were noted as being £4,373 2*s*. 4*d*., but it is not clear if this figure also covered improvements to transport facilities.

As the extension was in progress, the A.Y. Dinas Silica Brick & Lime Co. Ltd laid in a new siding on its railway alongside the brickworks and also relaid the

A view west from the top of Alexander Young's limekilns at Penymynydd Farm, 22nd September, 1994. *Author*

Alexander Young's limekilns, Penymynydd, 1971. Young's railway ran to the right of the hedge. Penymynydd Farm is behind the camera. *Roger Worsley*

Young's limekilns at Penymynydd Farm, and in the foreground the course of Young's railway. The track passed along this side of the hedge, climbing and curving towards the terminus at the farm. The small roofless structure is thought to have been an office. The level area behind the low stone wall was the site of the sidings. *Author*

Penymynydd Farm, Four Roads, 29th February, 1996. The east wall of the milking parlour, showing the original stonework of the locomotive shed, and the roof line as raised in 1978. As the height of the original would appear to have been no more than 15 ft (if that), it must have been a close fit for Young's engine. *Author*

Aerial view of Stephens & Co. Silica Brick Works, Kidwelly looking south-west, *c.* 1920s.
GWR Magazine

Aerial view of Stephens & Co. Silica Brick Works, Kidwelly looking north, *c.* 1930s.
Welsh Industrial & Maritime Museum

line for the half mile or more from the brickworks to Mynydd-y-Garreg. Whilst it was calculated that about 1,180 new sleepers would be needed for this task, it is not apparent that the company intended to buy new rail. By this time the track north of the brickworks to Penymynydd Farm was lightly used, and if any extra rail was required it might well have been available from one of the sidings at Penymynydd. Even so, it appears that the quarry at Penymynydd was reopened for a time in 1917, and at the same period it seems that a short narrow gauge tramway was put in between the brickworks and a sand and silica quarry near Graig Farm, just to the east. Much of this line was laid on an incline, intended to be self-acting in operation, but it is doubtful if it was much used. Although the technology for such an incline had existed for many years, it is believed that in this case the engineering was flawed, the gradient was too steep, and the line was beset by derailments.

In 1922, at the time of the GWR's take over of the GVR, these works - long known locally as 'Young's Brickyard' - were said to be in the hands of the Amalgamated Dinas Silica Brick Co. Ltd (note, no longer the A.Y. Dinas Silica & Lime Co.). The same report indicates that the works were out of use, and that there was then uncertainty about when they would be active again. In the event, it seems that the works never re-opened. According to one local legend the A.Y. Dinas Silica & Lime Co. was managed in its last years by a Scotsman who was distracted by drink. Whatever the truth of that may be, poor management appears to have been responsible for the failure of the company. It seems that the brickworks closed in 1921, but was kept intact for a few years in the hope of re-opening. The 1922 report suggests that rail traffic had then ceased. There is a local tradition that the very last bricks removed from the kilns were used in 1927 to complete the building of the Band Room for the once famous Mynydd-y-Garreg Silver Band. The Amalgamated Dinas Silica Brick Co. Ltd was wound up in the same year, and a suggestion that the business was taken over in 1929 by the local firm of Messrs H. & H.E.R. Smart has not been substantiated. Most of the equipment at Young's brickworks was sold at this period, although it is said that a number of the buildings were still standing at the time of World War II.

Stephens & Co., Brick and Limeworks

Before Daniel Stephens had acquired his lease of part of Mynydd-y-Garreg in 1895 he appears to have had control of a brickworks near the railway station at Kidwelly. North of the main line there was a small 'Dinas Silica Brickworks' at least as early as 1878, although this location is thought to have been the site of William Edwards' works, opened in 1858, and later continued by Messrs Frederick & Jenner. At all events, in or about 1903, Stephens & Co. decided to expand the brickworks on an open, largely green field site south of the South Wales main line close to Kidwelly station. More kilns were built, and a siding laid in from the South Wales main line. This was provided in 1904 to enable the works to receive limestone, sand and clay from the Mynydd-y-Garreg district, and also coal, as well as to dispatch bricks to steelworks and other customers, some of whom were as far afield as Scotland. At different dates no less than 20

Broomhill 0-4-0ST Peckett 1461/1917 seen in the yard of Thos Hall & Sons, Llansamlet in 1950, having been sold by Stephens Silica Brick Co. Ltd, Kidwelly in 1949.   *F. Jones*

A Stephens Silica Brick Co. Ltd private owner wagon at Kidwelly, 15th April, 1960. *J.A. Peden*

kilns were built at this works, but it is believed that a couple of the earlier, smaller kilns were demolished before the last three were built - numbers 18, 19 and 20. At its greatest extent, therefore, this brickworks had 18 operational, or potentially operational kilns, and found success at a time when some other brick producers, like Young's, were struggling.

Stephens & Co. had to pay the GWR for the right to bring wagons across the main line from the GWR on the north to its own sidings on the south. The wayleave was calculated on the basis that the wagons would be of a standard 10 tons capacity. After some time the chief proprietor, Sir Alfred Stephens, became dissatisfied because he felt the charge left very little room for profit. Accordingly he is reputed to have had larger wagons made, some timber built with a capacity of 15 tons, and some of steel construction with a capacity of 20 tons, thereby increasing the volume of raw materials he could bring in, and the quantity of bricks he could move out. These wagons were normally painted grey with white lettering and numbering.

In the early years of the brickworks it is not entirely clear what arrangements were in force for shunting and the movement of rail traffic into and out of the premises. Clearly the company had a working agreement with the GVR to bring raw materials down to Kidwelly, but the GVR locomotives were not officially registered with GWR to cross the main line until 1911. It is very possible that they did so anyway, because otherwise it must be imagined that a GWR engine played a part in the proceedings, and it seems improbable to suppose that the GW conceded to the GVR any arrangement which involved handling traffic over Great Western tracks. Even so, it is known that the railways did not have a monopoly of traffic. Even after World War I it is said there were some deliveries of silica stone by horse and cart from the quarries at Mynydd-y-Garreg.

Whatever the precise arrangements in this early period, in 1910 the brickworks company invested in a locomotive of its own, acquiring an outside cylinder 0-4-0ST built by Peckett & Co. of Bristol (No. 1247 of 1910). This engine was given the name *Barbara Cripps*, allegedly after Sir Alfred Stephens' married daughter. During World War I a very similar saddle tank locomotive was obtained from the same source, and *Barbara Cripps* was sent away to Lancashire to work for the Ministry of Munitions at Sutton Oak, near St Helens. The new engine was Peckett No. 1461 of 1917; it was named *Broomhill* after Sir Alfred Stephens' house.

Some 30 years later the company purchased another similar engine from Peckett & Co. This locomotive (No. 2082 of 1947) was named very appropriately *Sir Alfred*. In 1949 this acquisition was deemed sufficient for the company's Kidwelly site, and *Broomhill* was disposed of to Thomas Hall & Son, plant and machinery dealers at Llansamlet, near Swansea. In 1955 the Western Region of British Railways registered *Sir Alfred* as authorised to work across the South Wales main line (registration No. 882). Compared to its predecessors, however, this engine did not have a long life. In 1965 Stephens' Kidwelly brickworks was closed, and *Sir Alfred* was scrapped in August of the following year. The site of the brickworks has now been completely cleared, and is no more than a field of scrub providing grazing for ponies.

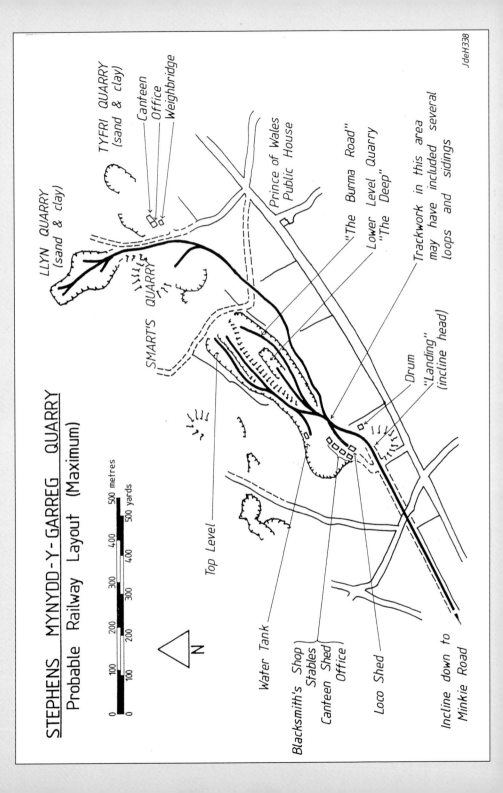

STEPHENS MYNYDD-Y-GARREG QUARRY
Probable Railway Layout (Maximum)

N

scale: 0 100 200 300 400 500 metres
0 100 200 300 400 500 yards

LLYN QUARRY (sand & clay)

TYFRI QUARRY (sand & clay)

Canteen
Office
Weighbridge

SMART'S QUARRY

Prince of Wales Public House

"The Burma Road"

Lower Level Quarry "The Deep"

Trackwork in this area may have included several loops and sidings

Drum

"Landing" (incline head)

Top Level

Water Tank

Blacksmith's Shop
Stables
Canteen Shed
Office

Loco Shed

Incline down to Minkie Road

JdeH338

Stephens & Co., Mynydd-y-Garreg Quarries

These limestone and silica stone quarries are believed to have been opened just before World War I. They were located high up on Mynydd-y-Garreg, about half a mile above 'the sidings' (or Minkie Road) and to the west of the main road from Kidwelly to Four Roads and Meinciau. A 2 ft 6 in. gauge tramway was laid in the quarry, together with a self-acting incline to take the drams down to a wharf alongside the Gwendraeth Valleys Railway at Minkie Road. A bridge over the incline carried the date of its construction (1914), and in the 1990s there were still one or two elderly local residents who could remember being taken as schoolchildren to see the first run of drams on the incline.

Broadly speaking, the north-west side of the quarries worked limestone, whilst to the south and east the emphasis was on silica stone or sand. From the top of the incline one rail track was laid close to the western extremity of the quarries, climbing up to a level known as '2nd floor', and then further to a point known as 'top floor', within 20 ft of the lip of the quarry. Here quarrymen gained magnificent views over the workings and across the countryside beyond.

The silica stone was of two kinds, referred to by the men as white ('gwyn') or red ('coch'). For many years it was the practice to produce a mixture of the two, but then the seam of red stone was lost. In an endeavour to recover it the workmen excavated a lower level in the heart of the quarries. This effort was sufficiently successful to justify the laying of a rail track down to this level, which was officially known as New Quarry, but referred to by the men as 'The Deep'. In the early years two or three horses were stabled on the site to haul drams within the quarries, and an ostler was appointed to look after them. Working the quarries was always a labour intensive operation, and at one time some 50 people were employed. Later, by 1949, the number had dropped to about forty.

It was realised that north-east of the main quarries were to be found further outcrops of silica stone, sand and clay, and very soon a silica working, known as Tyfri Quarry, was opened up just to the west of the main road, at a spot known locally as 'Queen Shop', north of 'The Prince of Wales' public house. The railway was extended up to these workings by a length of line which later became known as 'The Burma Road'. As the distance from the top of the incline to this area was about mile, in 1925 the decision was taken to introduce a steam locomotive.   The merits of this investment became evident in the easier movement of drams from the quarries to the incline head, and in improving access to other mineral deposits situated further to the north. Indeed, in due course it was decided to extend the line another few hundred yards to the north-east to reach silica sand and clay in a new working known as the Llyn Quarry. At its greatest extent, therefore, this line was about a mile long.

The working day began at 7.30 am and finished at 4.30 pm, and for most of the men it was a time of heavy work in extremely dusty conditions. Many were members of the Transport & General Workers Union, but union activity appears to have been slight. The first foreman was an ex-policeman named David

Peckett 1693 of 1925 working at Stephens' quarry, Mynydd-y-Garreg. Note the sacking to give protection to the locomotive driver, and the small tank wagon behind, believed to be for carrying water.

F. Jones

A group of quarrymen gather around Peckett 1693 of 1925 soon after it arrived new at Stephens & Co. quarry at Mynydd-y-Garreg. *Author's Collection*

Peckett 1693/1925 at Stephens Silica Brick Co. quarries at Mynydd-y-Garreg on 10th June, 1948. *J.A. Peden*

The 2 ft 6in. gauge Peckett 1693 at Mynydd-y-Garreg in 1950.   *F. Jones*

Peckett 2102 of 1949 at Stephens Silica Brick Co. quarries at Mynydd-y-Garreg in August 1953.
      F. Jones

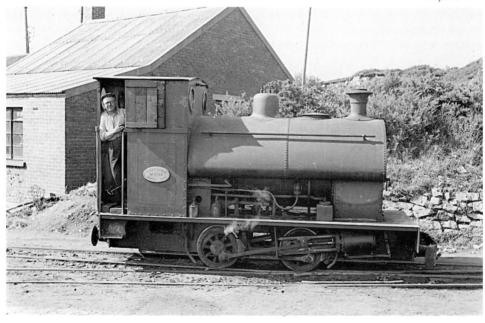

Peckett 1693 of 1925 dumped out of use at Stephens' quarry, Mynydd-y-Garreg, 1953. *F. Jones*

Peckett 1693 is seen once again, this time giving a good view of the footplate, as it lies out of use on 4th August, 1954. *D.L. Chatfield*

A view of the 2 ft 6 in. gauge system at Stephens' quarries, Mynydd-y-Garreg in 1954.

D.L. Chatfield

The working face of a quartzite quarry. Basal grit, Mynydd-y-Garreg *c*. 1956.

Quartzite quarry. Basal grit, Mynydd-y-Garreg, *c*. 1956.

Above: The strange landscape of Mynydd-y-Garreg: the abandoned Llyn Quarry on 22nd September, 1994.   *Author*

Right: The entrance to the former Tyfri Quarry at Mynydd-y-Garreg, showing the end wall of the office/mess building, and the site of the weighbridge, 29th February, 1996.   *Author*

Below: The brick-built office and mess shed at Tyfri Quarry, Mynydd-y-Garreg. The site of the weighbridge can be seen to the left of the building, and the former Smart's Quarry is to the extreme left, 29th February, 1996.   *Author*

Richards, who enjoyed considerable respect. Other notable characters included Edgar Anthony, the locomotive driver from 1926 to 1939, and David Davies, the ganger in charge of track maintenance. The vitally important post of 'incliner' or brakesman was held by Davey John Gravell. He occupied the winding house at the head of the incline and controlled the winding drum, and the brake, which was made largely of wood, was applied by a wheel.

In addition to the winding house there was near the incline top a blacksmith's shop, a workmen's cabin, an office, a stone-built engine shed and a corrugated-iron store shed. The incline was worked on a 'main and tail' basis, the usual practice being to send down five loaded drams, the weight of which would help to haul five empties up. The drams were coupled by three or four shackles, together with a coupling pin. There were three rails down the incline, the centre rail being common except at the passing loop between the overbridges where four rails were provided. At the foot of the incline a couple of short sidings were provided, together with a water supply. This was required to enable a man to hose down the limestone to inhibit dust before the stone was tipped into the railway wagons alongside the wharf on the GVR.

Several runaways occurred on this incline, one being when five drams went down unattached to the rope and crashed off the track at the passing loop. It is said that on at least two occasions at an earlier date drams careered down the full length of the incline, and plunged over the wharf onto the Gwendraeth Valleys Railway. Unfortunately no documentary evidence has come to light to support these stories, although such spectacular events would undoubtedly be memorable! Quite apart from these occurrences, overloaded drams would frequently shed stone as they descended, and clog the operation of the incline rope. In this event men would be sent down to clear and repair the track, but this was not a popular task. One of the workmen was normally quite silent, but under these circumstances even he could be stirred into speech!

The total number of drams in use varied somewhat during the life of the railway, but it is thought that about 60 brown, wooden bodied drams were built, each having a capacity of about 1¾ tons. In addition a water tank with a capacity of some 300 gallons was mounted on a suitable underframe and made available for use with the locomotive. A suggestion that there may also have been a small rail-mounted hand crane is still unsubstantiated. Meanwhile, in accordance with the custom of Stephens & Co., the locomotive was supplied by Peckett & Co. of Bristol, Works No. 1693 of 1925. It was painted green. By the end of World War II this engine was becoming worn, and it was decided to order another, slightly more powerful locomotive from Peckett & Co. This was Works No. 2102 of 1949, and after it arrived at Mynydd-y-Garreg the older engine was kept as a spare. By 1955 it was derelict, and it was scrapped.

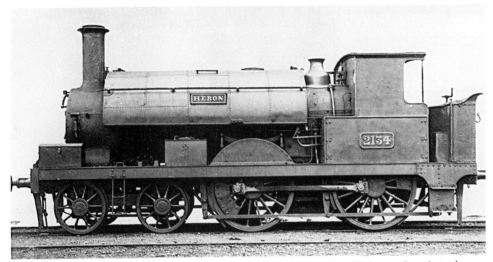

4-4-0T built by Sharp, Stewart & Co. for the Carmarthen & Cardigan Railway. On sale to the South Devon Railway in 1872 it was altered from a side tank to a saddle tank, and given the name *Heron*. It is seen here carrying the GWR number 2134. *Author's Collection*

4-4-0ST *Etna* built by Rothwell & Co. for the Carmarthen & Cardigan Railway, which, like *Heron*, later became the property of the South Devon Railway, and thereafter numbered 2132 by the GWR. *L&GRP*

Chapter Eight

Locomotives and Rolling Stock

Broad Gauge

After 1861 the Carmarthen & Cardigan Railway is known to have had the use of four broad gauge tank locomotives. Two of these were built by Sharp, Stewart & Co. in 1861 as 4-4-0 side tanks, builder's Nos. 1246/7. The engines had domeless boilers, 5 ft 2 in. coupled wheels, and cylinders measuring 17 in. x 24 in. During the financial confusion of the mid-1860s it seems they left the railway for a short period, but had been reinstated to traffic by June 1866. In 1872, after the gauge conversion in South Wales, they were sold to the South Devon Railway, and very promptly converted into saddle tanks, and given the names *Magpie* and *Heron*.

The other two engines were always typical broad gauge saddle tanks, and somewhat similar in size to the Sharp, Stewart locomotives. This pair were built by Rothwell & Co. of Bolton in 1864, and are believed to have been the last engines to have been constructed by this company. They were equipped with driving wheels measuring 5 ft 3 in. and cylinders of 17 in. x 24 in. dimensions. In due course they acquired the splendid names of *Etna* and *Hecla*. In February 1865, when the company's finances were in a state of almost indescribable chaos, these engines were sold, and then hired back from the purchasers. The fact that they never left the C&CR implies that the purchasers were sympathetic to the insolvent railway, and possibly near at hand - in brief, supporters of the company. The most likely explanation is that they were acquired by the contractor, H.A. Holden, because there is evidence that he worked the railway on behalf of the company after the sale of all its plant and rolling stock was ordered in November 1865. According to the records of the RCTS, the Rothwell locomotives were advertised for sale in June 1866, which corresponds with the return of the Sharp, Stewart engines to the railway. In the event *Etna* was not sold to the South Devon Railway until December 1868, and *Hecla* did not follow until December 1872.

Broad gauge locomotives generally had a size to match their gauge, and certainly none of these tank locomotives could really be described as 'small'. Accordingly the minutes of the C&CR Board meeting of 14 August, 1865, pose something of a mystery. In the minutes reference is made to letters from the Receiver, Mr Howe, and Messrs Everitt & Lucas, requesting 'that the small locomotive from Kidwelly be sent away from Kidwelly to Carmarthen'. This 'small locomotive' must have been either owned by the C&CR, or perhaps by Mr Holden on its behalf. However, in 1865 the broad gauge was barely a quarter of a century old, and hardly any locomotives had been sold out of service by main line companies to smaller concerns. Even so, there were a number of broad gauge contractors' locomotives in existence, and whilst there is no certain information available, it may be noted that Brotherhood & Co. of Chippenham are thought to have been disposing of engines of this type at this period.

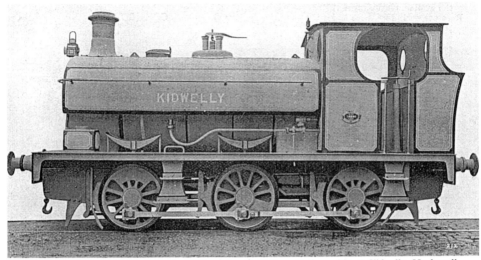

An official builder's photograph of Gwendraeth Valleys Railway No. 1 *Kidwelly*, Hudswell, Clarke No. 721 of 1905. This locomotive was also known as *Velindre*.   *F.K. Davies Collection*

GVR No. 1, HC 721 of 1905, pictured in June 1926, running as GWR No. 26 at Kidwelly.
F.K. Davies Collection

Whilst moving in the realms of speculation, there is one other point to be made. As there is evidence of the Gwendraeth Valleys Railway being operated at Kidwelly in the period 1866-1868/9, it must be assumed that some motive power was available for the purpose. Even though the 'small locomotive' was ordered away, the possibility may still exist of one of the Carmarthen & Cardigan engines being hired or borrowed for the purpose. If the two Rothwell engines were the property of H.A. Holden, when Holden was the contractor at work on the Carmarthen & Cardigan at Kidwelly, it seems more likely that a Rothwell locomotive was used there. Having been offered for sale in 1866, the *Etna* was sold in December 1868. Why was this engine disposed of before the *Hecla*? No doubt a number of explanations are possible, but if the *Etna* had been at Kidwelly, it could have been quite simply that when traffic ceased on the broad gauge GVR, there was no more work for it to do.

Unfortunately almost nothing is known of the rolling stock in use on the railway at this period. In 1864 the unsatisfactory books of the C&CR reveal regular rental payments to the Midland Wagon Co., presumably in respect of wagons. In October 1865 the C&CR Board received a letter, apparently from a Mr Worsdell of Birmingham, declining 'to repurchase the steam cranes at Kidwelly'. The company Secretary was instructed to advertise this equipment for sale in the newspapers.

Standard Gauge

No information has come to light concerning the motive power and plant employed in relaying the GVR as a standard gauge line. It is known that in 1872 a locomotive was supplied to the GVR by the Bristol firm of Fox, Walker & Co. This 0-6-0 saddle tank engine was Fox, Walker's No. 150 of 1872, and had 3 ft 6 in. wheels and cylinders measuring 13 in. x 20 in. Named *Kidwelly*, for the best part of four years it seems to have coped with all traffic alone. In 1876, however, it is believed that train services were entrusted to the neighbouring Burry Port & Gwendraeth Valley Railway which operated the *Kidwelly* for a sum varying upon the volume of traffic. Eventually, in or by 1884, the BP&GVR paid £1,000 for the engine, and took it into its own stock.

With one gap, the BP&GV remained in charge of traffic working on the GVR until 1905. In this period *Kidwelly* is thought to have been the most frequent performer on the GVR, although there is a brief reference in the papers of the BP&GVR to the Receiver of that company, John Russell, carrying out an inspection of the GVR with the aid of a locomotive named *Susan*, later renamed *Burry Port*. This was an 0-6-0 saddle tank, built by Manning, Wardle & Co. of Leeds, Works No. 459 of 1874, which came to the BP&GV from colliery service in June 1886.

Given the gradients up to Mynydd-y-Garreg, and the somewhat erratic traffic flows on this modest mineral line, it is considered unlikely that the BP&GV would have sent its most modern engines across to the GVR. If this assumption is correct, the most likely visitors besides those mentioned already would have been two more 0-6-0 saddle tanks, the *Cwm Mawr* and the *Dyvatty*. The former

GVR No. 1 as GWR No. 26, in the yard of A.R. Adams & Co., Newport, c. 1931, prior to sale for further use in South America.

F.K. Davies Collection

GVR No. 2 *Margaret* in steam at Kidwelly Tinplate Works. The engineman on the right is Phil Davies.

A. Lewis

An official builder's picture of Peckett 498 of 1891 supplied to the Burry Port & Gwendraeth Valley Railway and named *Dyvatty*. This engine is believed to have been used by the BP&GVR on the Gwendraeth Valleys line; it is not known whether it later became the property of Alexander Young, even though he is said to have had an engine 'Dyvatty'.   *F. Jones*

A BP&GVR visitor to the Gwendraeth Valleys Railway - the Avonside 0-6-0ST No. 2176 (formerly *Pembrey*) at Llanelly.   *F. Jones*

was another Manning, Wardle product, Works No. 731 of 1891, which saw service in industry before moving to Burry Port in 1894. It stayed on the BP&GV for 10 years before being sold to the Avonside Engine Co., of Bristol in part exchange for a new engine which was given the same name. *Cwm Mawr* quickly moved on to the Weston, Clevedon & Portishead Railway, where it was renamed *Weston*. The *Dyvatty* was built by Peckett & Co. of Bristol, Works No. 498 of 1891. This engine appears to have been a poor specimen, spending a considerable part of 1893 out of use on account of boiler defects. Although these were rectified, *Dyvatty* was never regarded with much enthusiasm, and was sold in November 1906. By that time there had been a clear-out of older engines, the sales including *Burry Port* in June 1901, *Kidwelly* in November 1902, and *Cwm Mawr* in August 1904.

The one gap in BP&GV working occurred in 1899, when presumably that company was suffering from a shortage of motive power. At all events, the company papers show that in the first half of 1899 Alexander Young & Co. were paid for working GVR traffic, and that in the second half of 1899 the task was shared between Alexander Young's engine and the BP&GVR.

By 1905 the time was ripe for improved motive power for the GVR. Following the company's change of management at this time the link between the new Chairman, Col J.R. Wright, and the Port Talbot Railway (PTR) seems to have been extremely useful. First, the GVR hired the locomotive *Penylan* from the PTR for much of 1905. Built by Manning, Wardle & Co. (Works No. 955) in 1886 for the Cardiff-based railway contractor J.E. Billups, it was part of the stock of the Cefn & Pyle Railway when that line was taken over by the Port Talbot Railway on 1st January, 1897. Another 0-6-0ST, this engine had cylinders of 14 in. x 20 in., and wheels of 3 ft 6 in..

Second, Col Wright is believed to have been influential in the purchase of a Hudswell, Clarke locomotive when new, or almost new, for £1,260. It has been said that this engine came to the GVR in late February 1905, through the good offices of the PTR, but the Hudswell, Clarke order book records delivery to the Kidwelly Tinplate Co. The builder's official photograph shows it carrying the very familiar name of *Kidwelly*, but before long it was referred to as the *Velindre*. An 0-6-0 saddle tank with cylinders measuring 14 in. x 20 in., wheel diameters of both 3 ft 7 in. and 3 ft 3½ in. have been noted. According to the Hudswell, Clarke order book it was to be painted in a dark green livery, with black, chrome and vermilion lining. It would appear that this locomotive was regarded as a special design because when in 1906 the builders received an order for a similar locomotive for a Yorkshire colliery it was referred to as a 'Kidwelly' class engine. As mentioned the GWR seems to have seen the GVR after 1905 as an industrial undertaking and the engines of the GVR had to be registered if working over Great Western tracks, as at Kidwelly. Accordingly in March 1911, *Velindre* became No. 74 on the register.

At a GVR Board meeting held on 8th June, 1909, the question of purchasing another locomotive was discussed - surely an indication of improving fortunes. The Chairman declared that he would be visiting Paddington shortly, and 'would see what he could do in the way of purchasing a second-hand locomotive from the GWR Co'. In fact almost a full year elapsed before such a

GVR No. 2 *Margaret* outside the locomotive shed at Kidwelly Tinplate Works, 26th June, 1955.
F.K. Davies

GVR No. 2/GWR No. 1378 at Scolton Manor Museum in September 1981.   *Author*

purchase took place, but on 21st June, 1910, Col Wright announced that he had agreed the purchase of the second-hand locomotive *Margaret* No. 1378, offered by the GWR for £800 delivered at Kidwelly. He added that the agreement provided for 'the engine to be fitted with new tyres on all wheels, and one new steam brake, and to be put in good working order by the GWR Co. before delivery'.

The *Margaret* had been built in 1878 by Fox, Walker & Co. of Bristol, Works No. 410, for the Maenclochog Railway (later the North Pembrokeshire & Fishguard Railway), an impecunious undertaking operating across the southern slopes of the Prescelli hills in Pembrokeshire. In July 1898 this company was taken over by the Great Western, and its stock incorporated with that of the GWR. As 0-6-0ST No. 1378, *Margaret* was rebuilt at Swindon in 1904. It had inside cylinders measuring 16 in. x 22 in., and 4 ft 0 in. wheels; the total heating surface was now 892.94 sq. ft and the boiler pressure 1401b. The capacity of the saddle tank was 500 gallons, and the total weight 30 tons 19 cwt. After arrival at Kidwelly *Margaret* became GVR No. 2, whilst *Velindre* became GVR No. 1. In January 1911, the *Margaret* became No. 73 in the register of engines allowed to work over Great Western metals. Whilst in Gwendraeth Valleys service both locomotives were painted dark green, with polished brass fittings.

When the GVR was absorbed into the Great Western at the beginning of 1923, the new owners soon demonstrated their reluctance to have anything to do with the *Margaret*. In March 1923 it was sold to the Kidwelly Tinplate Co., quite possibly without having left the Gwendraeth Valleys line. The *Velindre* fared better, being allocated the Great Western No. 26. However, by June 1926, it had been deprived of its name even though it was then still working at Kidwelly. Soon afterwards it was moved to Neath, where it had a spell as shed pilot. This engine was withdrawn from service in December 1927, and sold to Charles Williams of Morriston in the following month. On the closure of his business in 1931 the locomotive was sold to A.R. Adams of Newport, before being resold to the Anglo-Scottish Construction Co., for use on a contract in South America. The eventual fate of *Velindre* is not known, although it is thought to have been active in Uruguay in 1935.

Rolling Stock

Little is known of the GVR's rolling stock. Between 1885 and the end of 1896 the half-yearly returns refer to '25 goods wagons'. Thereafter, if the records are to be believed, the company owned no stock of its own until 1906. The minutes of a Board meeting held on 12th September that year offer a possible explanation by mentioning the use of private owner wagons. On this occasion it was resolved that the GVR 'take over the wagons of the Tinplate company, consisting of 10 covered vans and 10 opens, at the price at which they stood in the books of the Tinplate company on 30th June, 1906 - viz, £606 13s. 4d. The half-yearly report for the period to 31st December, 1906, mentions 10 covered vans (four of which are on redemption) and 20 open wagons'. Somewhat surprisingly, no mention of brakevans has been seen, and although the BP&GVR used brakevans it has been alleged that in the Kidwelly Tinplate Co. era after 1905 the company chose to operate in the same way as many industrial undertakings, by working trains without brakevans. Whether the Board of Trade would have approved of such a practice is very doubtful, but as the Board of Trade seems to be unaware of the GVR's activities the issue remains unresolved. Suffice to say that there is a strong tradition in the district that local people could get lifts on the train by riding with the guard. In GWR days trains undoubtedly operated with brakevans.

The only change in the ensuing years came in 1916, when the number of open wagons owned by the GVR dropped to 19 very probably as a result of one being lost in an accident. The 10 ton covered vans were numbered between 11 and 20, whilst the opens are all believed to have carried numbers between 51 and 70. Although the GVR's own returns mention 19 open wagons right up to the time of the company's take over by the GWR, the stock records from Swindon mention only 12 open wagons, all withdrawn quickly in 1923. Seven of these were 10 ton wagons (Nos. 51, 53, 55, 56, 62, 64, and 66) and five were 8 ton wagons (Nos. 60, 61, 63, 65, 69). The last GVR rolling stock to be withdrawn were of the two covered vans, Nos. 16 and 19, on 29th December, 1923.

Tinplate workers in the 1920s. *Author's Collection*

Chapter Nine

The Final Years

The Great Western's take over of the GVR had the effect of rolling the clock back 20 years to the time when the line was worked by the BP&GVR. After June 1923, when the locomotive shed at Kidwelly was officially closed, the motive power was provided by the shed at Burry Port, and some of the enginemen of the former BP&GV were enabled to renew their acquaintance with the line. Initially the Gwendraeth Valleys locomotive *Velindre*, now GWR No. 26, remained active at Kidwelly, and it has been suggested that it continued to use the small locomotive shed for some time after official closure. This may be so, because there is some anecdotal evidence to support the belief that the shed was still used from time to time for the stabling of a spare engine. At all events, the other GVR locomotive, the *Margaret* appears to have been confined to the sidings at the tinplate works following its sale to the Tinplate Co. in March 1923. At the same time it seems to found new company in the form of another 0-6-0 saddle tank. In late 1922 or early 1923 the Kidwelly Tinplate Co. acquired an engine built by Hudswell, Clarke & Co., Works No. 1283 of 1917, from a Ministry of Munitions depot at Coventry. No name is recorded, but as suggested in the previous chapter, it is just possible that this engine carried the name 'Dyvatty' for some time. It is believed to have left Kidwelly before 1930 for further work with Evan Davies & Co. at Crown colliery, Pwll, west of Llanelli.

In the 1920s the Great Western made considerable use of the spur from Tycoch Junction to the South Wales main line for coal traffic out from the Gwendraeth Fawr valley, and consignments of pit timber into it. Although the BP&GVR had had a platform for colliers' trains adjoining the junction at Tycoch since 1899 (and possibly earlier), it seems that it may not have been given a building before 1909, when the well known light railway engineer Col H.F. Stephens was engaged in the reconstruction of the BP&GVR as a passenger line. At all events, the small ticket office was a simple structure in the Col Stephens' style, and it was manned in the early mornings. Presumably because it was not advertised in a public timetable it was not given much attention by the GWR, but its existence was well known locally. In effect Tycoch became a second station for Kidwelly, the trains being operated on weekdays only, ostensibly for colliers, but in practice for anyone who cared to travel. Rather curiously, the working timetables referred to this location as Tycoch Platform, whilst the GWR's printed tickets described it as Tycoch Halt. As much of the BP&GVR had been laid either on the towpath or on the bed of earlier canals some sections of line were very susceptible to flooding. In winter the track at Tycoch could become swamped, but one of the most troublesome spots was further north at Glyn Abbey. On one occasion the morning workmen's train was stopped here by flood water, and compelled to return to Tycoch - giving the colliers and others a day off!

Whilst mentioning Tycoch, it is appropriate to make brief mention of the

Tinplate workers.   *Author's Collection*

Taking a break from the heat of Kidwelly Tinplate Works: a group of workmen *c.* 1930.

Author's Collection

former BP&GVR line from Tycoch to Kidwelly Quay. By World War I the continuing silting of the river estuary had severely restricted access for shipping to the quay, and traffic over the railway to the quay dropped off. Thereafter it was used only for a few occasional wagon loads of coal to be transferred into small vessels at the quay. In the 1920s the track became heavily overgrown, and the cost of renovating the line was felt to be out of all proportion to the traffic carried. Accordingly this section from Tycoch to the quay was closed in October 1929, and it was eventually lifted in 1933.

By 1926 the BP&GVR's own coaching stock had been withdrawn, and replaced by 4-wheel coaches, mostly of GWR origin. Whilst there is no documentary evidence of any kind of passenger service being operated between Kidwelly and Mynydd-y-Garreg, tales are told locally of coaching stock being in use on the Gwendraeth Valleys line at this period. Two residents claimed to remember passengers waving to them as boys playing by the lineside! As the Great Western was not a company to flout official regulations, such tales seem intrinsically improbable, although they might tie in with a recollection of a couple of primitive oil-lit, 4-wheel coaches being stabled at Kidwelly for a time in the 1930s. The only likely explanation would seem to be that the local men had witnessed the passing of one of the Great Western's own inspection trains.

Although Young's brickworks (then known as the Amalgamated Dinas Silica Brickworks) north of Mynydd-y-Garreg, closed in 1921, the Smart's Brickworks, just north of the main road through Kidwelly, fared better. The firm was reconstituted as Smart's Dinas Silica Brick Co. by 1930, in June of which year a new private siding agreement was signed with the GWR. At the same period, in August 1930, the GWR also entered into a new private siding agreement with the Stephens Silica Brick Co. Ltd in respect of their stone loading wharf at Minkie Road sidings. A couple of years later, in December 1928, another source of traffic appeared when the GWR concluded an agreement to serve the private siding at Kidwelly Gasworks, located by the short length of line from Kidwelly to Tycoch Junction. Overall these developments indicated more business for the railway at Kidwelly, whilst traffic at Mynydd-y-Garreg remained variable.

In the 1930s the Kidwelly tinplate works was struggling to survive, and finding it difficult to cope with rapidly increasing competition. Tinplate manufacture was subject to numerous interruptions, and many tinworkers experienced periods of unemployment. By 1932 only John Thomas of the original Board members of the Kidwelly Tinplate Co. was still in office, serving still as Managing Director. The company Chairman was now Frederick J. Rees, who had joined the Board during World War I.

In these uncertain years tinplate workers and their families used to look out for the trains climbing up to Mynydd-y-Garreg. If they could see consignments of steel ingots it meant that they had work; if there was no steel lay-offs were likely. Alternatively, if the works had been 'on stop' steel ingots represented a re-opening - so the steel was always good news. At busy times the weight of these ingots was such that it might be necessary to divide the train at Kidwelly before working it forward to Mynydd-y-Garreg in two parts. According to some railwaymen's recollections, the tinworks was usually served by a train working up after 9.00 am, having arrived at Kidwelly from Burry Port at about

Top, left: D. Gravell, GWR at Mynydd-y-Garreg and Minkie Road *c*. 1930s. Note the weighbridge at Minkie Road sidings in the background.   *Eric Hughes*

Top, right: Railwaymen take a break between duties at Mynydd-y-Garreg. The GWR pannier tank locomotive is standing at 'The sidings'.   *L. Francis*

Below: Railwaymen at Kidwelly with GWR 0-6-0ST No. 1957 *c*. 1948. *Left to right*: guard, Dan Gravell; driver, W.E. Evans; unknown; shunter, William Morris.   *L. Francis*

8.00 am. Unfortunately no working timetables for the 1920s have come to light, so the official timings of trains are not known. In the ordinary course of events, though, there was only one train a day to shunt at Kidwelly, and to serve Smarts', Stephens', the tinplate works and the Kidwelly gasworks.

As the tinplate industry continued to experience difficulties, several firms in Carmarthenshire eventually recognised the need to seek security through amalgamation. In April 1939 the Kidwelly works (with a number of others) was taken over by the newly formed Llanelly Associated Tinplate Co. Ltd, and it ceased to trade as a separate business. The hope was that this larger company would be able to find the resources to build a truly modern tinplate works to meet foreign competition. Unfortunately an initial shortage of capital somewhat dampened expectations, before the onset of World War II put a stop to the scheme. As government policy did not favour the tinplate industry, production was restricted and there was a spate of works' closures early in the war. Although the GWR signed a private siding agreement with the new company in April 1940, it did not prosper. Indeed, the whole enterprise was under-funded, and the Kidwelly works continued to struggle. It closed eventually in July 1941, and although all the machinery was left in place, the site was promptly taken over by the Ministry of Supply as a secure storage depot for everything from tobacco to motor vehicle spares. By 1942 the *Margaret* had been stored out of use in its shed.

Whilst the last years of the tinplate works saw erratic flows of traffic to and from Mynydd-y-Garreg, it is believed that for two or three years after 1941 the traffic was steady but modest. In 1943 there was an additional development at Mynydd-y-Garreg when Rees Jones of Bridgend, proprietor of a company called Rock Products Ltd, completed a private siding agreement for the Great Western to transport both lime and limestone. This company, which had a stake in the limestone quarries further north at Van, made use of a siding near the foot of the huge limekilns of 1872, actually employing some of the kilns to produce lime. Before the end of World War II, this operation had been taken over by a Kidwelly businessman, Tom Gravell, who also had an interest in the limeworks at Van.

Given that the main business of the Mynydd-y-Garreg line was to serve three or four particular customers along the route, it has never been entirely clear how much agricultural and other goods traffic was carried. Certainly the two sidings which were described as the Mynydd-y-Garreg goods depot had little storage provision, and in October 1946 it was officially closed. Two years later the nearby tinplate works was taken over by Messrs J.& P. Zammit, who seem to have specialised in dealing in WD surplus stores and equipment, and in scrap metal. A private siding agreement with J. & P. Zammit Ltd. was signed on 4th September, 1950, and it is believed that occasional wagon loads of scrap were delivered to the site. Somewhat surprisingly, in view of Zammit's interest in the scrap business, the old machinery in the tinplate works was left untouched.

As road and bus services improved the number of colliers and others using the workmen's service from Tycoch declined, and the service was finally withdrawn in May 1949. The timber building was removed in about 1950, but sat in a field a few hundred yards away for many years afterwards. Soon after

GWENDRAETH VALLEY SECTION (TRIMSARAN ROAD TO KIDWELLY).
GENERAL WORKING ARRANGEMENTS.

Traffic over the Gwendraeth Valley Section, embracing the following sub-sections, is worked in accordance with the "Regulations for Working Single Lines of Railway by one Engine in steam, or two or more Engines coupled together", as shewn on pages 84 and 85 of the Regulations for Train Signalling :—

1.—Kidwelly to Mynydd-y-Garreg.
2.—Kidwelly to Kidwelly Junction.

A key is attached to the Staff for operating the Ground Frame at the Storage Sidings near Kidwelly Junction. Points at other places as well as the Wheel Blocks at Mynydd-y-Garreg are locked by ordinary padlocks.,

The Guard will be responsible for manipulating the Wheel Blocks and locking them across the rails ; also for placing all points in proper position and padlocking them on completion of work. The keys of the padlocks must be kept in Kidwelly Signal Box when not in use.,

The Signalman at Kidwelly Junction will be responsible for the safe custody of the Staff and keys when not in use, and an entry must be made in the Train Register Book shewing when the Staff is given out and when it is returned—the entry to be initialled by the Signalman, and by the person receiving the Staff and returning it to the Box.

MINKIE CROSSING, MYNYDD-Y-GARREG, NEAR KIDWELLY.

Gates have been provided at this crossing which are so hung that they will close automatically across the railway. Stop boards have also been provided on each side of the crossing, the one on the South side being 80 yards away, and the one on the North side being 50 yards away. All Trains and Engines must stop dead at these stop boards, and must not proceed beyond them until the Guard or Shunter in charge has gone to the crossing and placed and secured the gates across the roadway, after which he will give the necessary hand-signals to the Engine Driver.

In the case of a Light Engine, the Fireman must perform this duty.

After the Train or Engine has passed over the crossing, the gates must again be placed across the railway.

WORKING OF TRAINS AND LIGHT ENGINES—KIDWELLY YARD TO TYCOCH PLATFORM, AND VICE VERSA.

When a Train is allowed to travel over the Running Line between these points, the Guard or Shunter must satisfy himself that the hand points are properly set before hand-signalling the Driver to pass over them. In the case of a Light Engine, it is the duty of the Fireman to do so.

PROVISION OF WHEEL BLOCK, TYCOCH MILEAGE SIDING, KIDWELLY.

A Wheel Block is fixed at Tycoch Mileage Siding, Kidwelly (G.V. Section) and the key of the padlock on it will be kept with other keys used on the Gwendraeth Valley Section. Guards will be responsible for manipulating the Wheel Block and for placing it across the rail on completion of shunting operations.

INSTRUCTIONS FOR WORKING AT THE LIME KILN AND TIN WORKS SIDINGS, MYNYDD-Y-GARREG.

When shunting in the Lime Kiln and Tin Works Sidings at Mynydd-y-Garreg, an Engine or/and vehicles must not be permitted to remain stationary on or foul of the level crossing and wagons must not be gravitated over the Lime Kiln Siding for the purpose of being attached to an Engine, but the Engine must be brought up to the wagons to be attached.

INSTRUCTIONS FOR WORKING ON THE MYNYDD-Y-GARREG BRANCH.
MESSRS. H. and H. W. SMARTS BRICK WORKS NEAR KIDWELLY.

The connection with the above Siding is facing for Up Trains in the direction of Mynydd-y-Garreg, and wagons for the Siding must be propelled from Kidwelly Yard in clear weather and during daylight only. Not exceeding 6 wagons may be propelled at any one time, and the Guard must ride upon the leading vehicle, or precede the wagons on foot.

The Siding points are secured by padlock, and the Guard is responsible for their manipulation, in accordance with the instructions contained on page 329.

MINKIE LIMEKILNS, AND KIDWELLY TINPLATE WORKS SIDINGS.

Traffic for the Sidings serving the above must be propelled with Brake Van leading, in which the Guard must ride, keep a sharp look-out, and be prepared to hand-signal to the Driver as required.

The number of wagons propelled must not exceed 25 at any one time.

Trains must be brought to a stand 100 yards above Minkie, before reaching the change of gradient ; the Guard must then apply sufficient brakes on the leading vehicles, to ensure their being kept under control over the falling gradient.

The Guard must hand-signal to the Driver to stop short of the Shintor-fach public level crossing, which is situate near the connection leading to the Lower Limekiln Siding, and must exhibit an "All right" signal when he is satisfied that it is in order to do so. The Driver must not pass over the crossing until he has received the hand-signal from the Guard.

The Driver must whistle when approaching level crossings, and be prepared to act on **hand**-signals from the Guard.

After sunset, and during fog or falling snow, a white light must be exhibited on the leading end of the Brake Van.

When shunting in the above Sidings, an Engine or/and vehicles must not be permitted to remain stationary on or foul of the level crossing, and wagons must not be gravitated over the Limekilns Siding for the purpose of being attached to an Engine, but the Engine must be brought up to the wagons to be attached.

WHEEL BLOCK IN EMPTY COACH SIDING—KIDWELLY.

A wheel block is fixed at the Eastern end of the Empty Coach Siding, Kidwelly (Gwendraeth Valley Line), and the key of the padlock on it is kept with the Mynydd-y-Garreg Branch Keys. Guards are responsible for manipulating the wheel block, locking it across the rails on completion of shunting, and returning the key with others, to the Kidwelly Station Signal Box where they are kept when not in use.

Extract from GWR Swansea Division Appendix to Working Timetables, February 1939.

this service was withdrawn some thought was given to the possibility of closing the line from Kidwelly Junction on the BP&GV to Tycoch as an economy measure, diverting freight services to and from Kidwelly over the South Wales main line. In the event, nothing was done because of the desirability of maintaining the route for emergency use. On the line between Burry Port and Kidwelly Junction there were several low bridges, with severely restricted clearances. In the event of an emergency in the Gwendraeth valley requiring a breakdown crane the line from Tycoch offered the only means of access, and so was allowed to remain operational.

A railway as isolated and idiosyncratic as the Gwendraeth Valleys line was bound to have its share of amusing characters and incidents. Although under the GWR regime there was a man appointed to look after the level crossing, sidings and weighbridge at Minkie Road, his only means of communication with the outside world was a primitive telephone. This was used as required by other railway staff, not least train guards reporting progress or problems. One guard was blessed with the surname of Nott, and innocently caused confusion by ringing control and announcing 'This is Nott the guard speaking . . .' In common with many rural lines, train crews on this section enjoyed a leisurely life, with plenty of opportunities for conversation and cups of tea, or maybe something stronger. Given the chance, some were not averse to a little poaching, although their efforts did not always work out as planned. On one occasion, for example, the crew of an engine passing Waungadog Farm saw a fat chicken pecking away in the dust by the track. As a countryman the fireman knew what to do, and as soon as the train came to a halt he expertly seized the bird and stuffed it into the tool box on the side of the engine. By the time the train had reached Kidwelly the chicken had recovered from its shock, and began to protest. As the engine was shunting at the goods shed, between the passenger station and the level crossing on the main line, squeals were heard by a bemused station master. The enginemen hastily put the blower on, and made as much noise as possible. Only when they had backed out, and escaped to the safety of the gasworks siding did the fireman get down to look into the tool box. The wretched chicken had tipped over an oil can, and was completely covered in thick green oil. The only decent thing to do was to kill it as quickly as possible; it was no longer a meal for anyone.

On 1st January, 1948, the GWR became part of the newly nationalised British Railways. Accordingly all lines in the vicinity of Kidwelly and the Gwendraeth valley became part of the Western Region, although in practice there was virtually no change in the manner of their operation. In the summer of 1952 the weekday goods service for Kidwelly was due to leave Burry Port at 8.25 am, and after a nine minute stop at Kidwelly Junction reached the old GVR goods yard at Kidwelly soon after 9.00 am. The locomotive then worked as required at Kidwelly, and over the section to Mynydd-y-Garreg, before returning from Kidwelly Yard at 5.45 pm to reach Burry Port by 6.40 pm. On Saturdays the outward journey corresponded to the usual weekday timings, but the train was due to leave Kidwelly Yard at 3.00 pm and get back to Burry Port by 4.25 pm.

In the 1940s the customary motive power for the Kidwelly and Mynydd-y-Garreg trip was one of Burry Port's '850' class of 0-6-0 pannier tank engines,

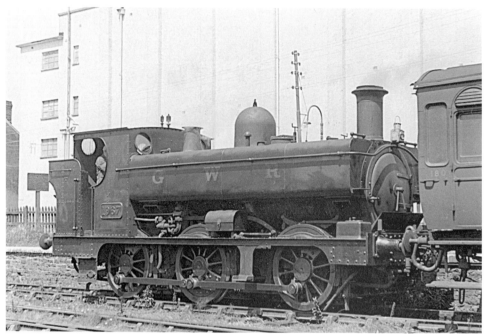

Several of this class of pannier tank visited Mynydd-y-Garreg. No. 1967 is seen here at Burry Port in 1947.   *H.C. Casserley*

A BP&GVR visitor to the Gwendraeth Valleys Railway - Hudswell, Clarke-built 0-6-0T No. 2198 seen at Llanelly.   *F. Jones*

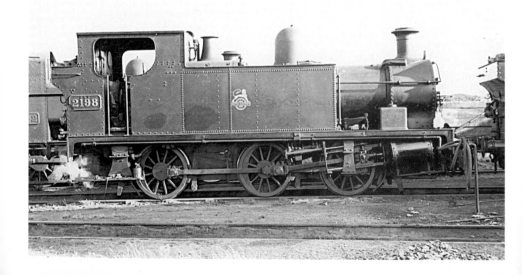

How many have such memories of childhood? BR 0-6-0PT No. 1644 at Burry Port shed in the summer of 1953; the locomotive was used on the GVR. *R. Daniells*

A '16XX' class 0-6-0PT, thought to be No. 1651, shunts at Kidwelly on 20th September, 1963. The wagon and brakevan standing beyond the gate are on the remaining track of the Gwendraeth Valleys Railway. *L. Francis*

Tycoch Halt, view looking north, 31st July, 1958. Compare this, with the 1993 view of the relaid line at this spot on page 114.   *M. Hale*

Tycoch Halt in August 1964, as nature takes over.   *Author*

although one of the surviving BP&GVR locomotives would quite often be employed. Occasionally a '2021' class pannier tank might be used, and Nos. 2026, 2027, 2065 and 2081 of this class are believed to have reached Kidwelly. The most commonly seen members of the '850' class were Nos. 1907, 1957, 1967, and 2012, but the Burry Port allocation at this period included Nos. 1909, 2002 and 2019, and there can be little doubt that they also worked to Mynydd-y-Garreg from time to time. The BP&GV engine most often seen was numbered 2198 by the GWR, although No. 2176 has been mentioned as a visitor, and doubtless there were others. No. 2198 actually outlived the other engines mentioned above, and also all other BP&GV locomotives, not being withdrawn until March 1957. By then the older GWR types had given way to a new design in the same Swindon-built tradition, in the shape of the '16XX' class of pannier tanks. Introduced in 1949, these engines soon appeared in West Wales in considerable numbers, and Llanelly shed was given a sizeable allocation. No doubt most if not all of these visited Kidwelly on occasions, but locomotives Nos. 1607, 1611, 1618, 1624, 1643, 1644, 1651 and 1666 are known to have put in appearances. Notwithstanding this new motive power, latterly only half a dozen wagons might be propelled up to the sidings, and there might be only four or five loaded wagons to remove. On returning to Kidwelly two or three wagons might be needed at Smart's, and a few more over the main line at Stephens'. The gasworks was shunted when required.

Notwithstanding this new motive power, the 1950s were years of decline for the former Gwendraeth Valleys Railway. At Mynydd-y-Garreg Tom Gravell decided to use road transport to the exclusion of rail in 1954, although the private siding agreement in the name of Rock Products Ltd was not formally terminated until 25th October, 1956. Gravell made considerable use of the 1872 limekilns, and when his business was at its peak each of the seven kilns could be producing as much as 27 tons of lime per day, giving a potential 15 or 16 wagon-loads per day for the railway. Almost all the lime went for agricultural purposes, but some kibbled lime (crushed limestone) found a market at the Elba steelworks, Gowerton, and at Bynea steelworks, east of Llanelly. Latterly all this trade was done by road. Nearby, at the Minkie Road sidings, the economics of the narrow gauge system at the Stephens' Silica Brick Co. quarries had also come into question, and regular traffic ended by September 1955. One source suggests that the track was lifted the same month, but other advice indicates that the task was not completed until 1956. The Peckett locomotive, Works No. 2102 was sold to R. & S. Hayes Ltd of Bridgend in 1955, and was eventually scrapped in August 1957. Meanwhile the standard gauge private siding agreement was eventually terminated on 16th August, 1957, and it is believed that rail traffic to Mynydd-y-Garreg was negligible thereafter, although some stone was still being extracted from the quarries and transported away by road. Tom Gravell's activity at Mynydd-y-Garreg finally ceased in 1960, on the withdrawal of a valuable government subsidy.

Matters were not much better at the Kidwelly end of the line. Smart's Dinas Silica Brick Co was in some difficulty, and closed by 1960. Although this firm was very probably the last on the 'main line' of the former GVR to see any rail traffic, the private siding agreement ceased with effect from 21st October, 1959.

Flooded track of the Gwendraeth Valley line at Tycoch, looking towards Kidwelly, August 1964.
Author

A scene in the yard at Burry Port in August 1964. Class '16XX' 0-6-0PT No. 1611 rests between shunting duties; the picture could very readily have been taken in the yard at Kidwelly a few years earlier.   *Author*

This was effectively the kiss of death for the Mynydd-y-Garreg line, because without commerce it could not survive. Officially this section was last used in February 1959, although it was not formally declared closed until August 1960. Even then it found another use, because for two or three years the line up to the level crossing at Minkie Road was used for storing redundant rolling stock. At one stage so many old vans and carriages were stabled on the railway that some of the more adventurous local lads reckoned it was possible to cover the entire distance climbing over the stock, without ever touching the ground! The rails beyond a point 15 chains north of the junction at Kidwelly are believed to have been lifted by the end of 1963.

The much shorter portion of the GVR to Tycoch lasted a little longer, carrying traffic to the main line until 1965. Kidwelly gasworks closed in about 1962, with the working agreement in respect of the gasworks siding ending that October. The siding was disconnected in November 1963. Stephens' Brickworks latterly operated 16 kilns, and was by far the largest brickworks at Kidwelly. In November 1955 their Peckett tank locomotive *Sir Alfred* was approved as fit to cross the South Wales main line to take traffic to and from Kidwelly Yard, thereby giving the firm greater flexibility of movement than could be provided by the one train a day from Burry Port. Unfortunately, trading conditions were becoming more hostile, and by the early 1960s the business was in trouble. Stephens' Brickworks closed down late in 1964, or early in 1965, and before the end of the year rail connections had been severed. Indeed, in October 1965, an already reduced Kidwelly Yard was closed completely, and the last remnants of the old GVR swept away. The bridge taking the GVR over the main road at Kidwelly was soon reduced to rubble, and Stephens' Brickworks demolished. The site of the brickworks was later completely cleared.

The two main industrial relics at Mynydd-y-Garreg - the Tinplate Works and Threlfall's limekilns - did not endure either. Unfortunately they were located in an area unaccustomed to addressing either the possibilities of tourism, or the claims of industrial history. Threlfall's magnificent kilns were thought to be more of a safety hazard than a potential asset, and in the early 1970s officialdom ordered demolition. The Tinplate Works fared only marginally better, because although in 1971 it was still amazingly intact, and barely altered in the 30 years since closure, someone decided upon selective demolition before the possibility of preservation was taken seriously. The essence of the site was its completeness; what then took place destroyed vital features like the tin house, and robbed the site of most of its interest. Fortunately one fine item was saved - the old GVR locomotive *Margaret*. In the early 1970s several people, including the present writer, had been in correspondence with Zammit's seeking to secure the locomotive for preservation. It was not until they found themselves in some financial trouble in 1974 that Zammit's decided to dispose of the whole site. After some very hasty negotiations, the engine was purchased for preservation at the Scolton Manor Museum in Pembrokeshire. In July 1974 the *Margaret* was retrieved from her shed by a working party, and taken west. The remains of the Tinplate Works were later adopted by more enlightened minds, and became the basis for the Kidwelly Industrial Museum, which opened to the public in 1987. However, the story of the old GVR was now clearly over.

Kilns built in 1872 by Edward Threlfall.   *Roger Worsley*

Margaret at Kidwelly Tinplate Works being hauled onto a low-loader in preparation for its journey to Scolton Manor Museum, 23rd June, 1974.   *F.K. Davies*

Chapter Ten

The Route Described

Kidwelly station on the South Wales main line is situated a fraction under 234½ miles from Paddington, the mileage being measured by the original route via Gloucester rather than the later route via the Severn Tunnel. The Gwendraeth Valleys Railway began just over a quarter of a mile east of the station, in sidings on the north side of the main line at 234 miles 10 chains. A home signal at this spot guarded access to the Great Western Railway; there was no signalling at all on the line to Mynydd-y-Garreg as this route was worked on the basis of 'one engine in steam'. A mere three chains (66 yards) up the GVR, at a point known as Tycoch Loop Junction, the spur to Tycoch on the Burry Port & Gwendraeth Valley Railway branched off to the east on an alignment virtually parallel with the main line. Almost immediately another set of points on the branch gave access to the GVR locomotive shed, situated on land between the lines to Mynydd-y-Garreg and Tycoch. Reputedly built in 1905, and measuring approximately 40 ft by 15 ft, the shed is believed to have been built in brick and stone, with a slate roof. The original shed on this site may have been slightly larger as it was erected in the broad gauge era. An early plan, now lost, not only showed this shed but also a block of coke ovens nearby. At this period it was standard practice for engines to be fuelled on coke, but it was not common to provide coke ovens adjacent to a shed, let alone a depot serving only one or two locomotives. The reasons are not clear, but it may well be supposed that these ovens were erected to provide coke for all Carmarthen & Cardigan locomotives, even though this would involve movement over part of the South Wales main line to reach Carmarthen. At all events, the GVR's broad gauge era was very brief, and as locomotive technology improved rapidly, coke became less important as a fuel. The Kidwelly coke ovens were soon removed, possibly even before the line was converted to the standard gauge.

The Tycoch branch to the junction with the BP&GVR was only about 530 yards long, although a GVR siding on the north side of the line at the junction extended GVR track by perhaps 10 yards. This siding was situated at a slightly higher level than the junction line, which had to drop down to meet the BP&GV line from Kidwelly Quay. In effect the siding was a survival from the earliest days, when broad gauge track had been laid to a wharf on the Kidwelly & Llanelly Canal. In the GVR's standard gauge days (and later) it is believed to have been used as a public coal yard, with a weighbridge near the main road. By 1880 the Tycoch branch running line was accompanied for most its length by a loop siding, and during the 1920s a short siding was laid in on the north side to serve the Kidwelly town gasworks.

The Mynydd-y-Garreg line curved away from the junction to the north on a gradient of 1 in 40. A quarter of a mile from the junction it crossed the main road from Pembrey to Kidwelly on a substantial stone arched bridge before passing Messrs Smart's silica brickworks on the east side of the line. The original siding serving these works was laid on the alignment of the abortive

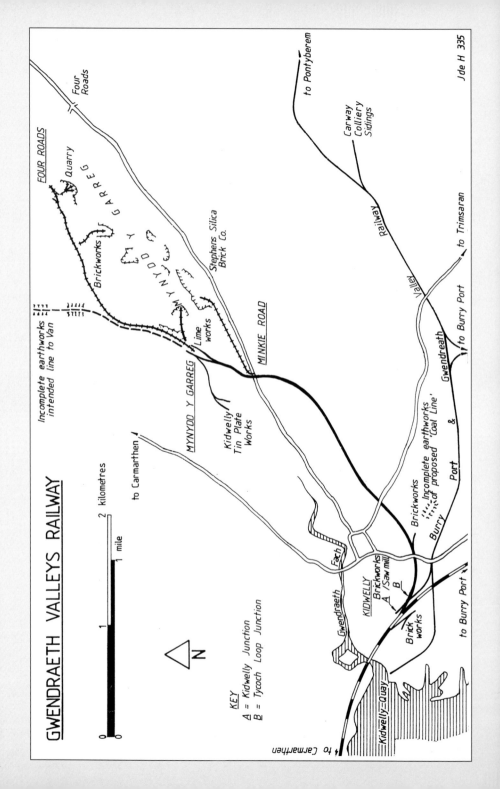

GWENDRAETH VALLEYS RAILWAY

2 kilometres

1 mile

N

KEY
A = Kidwelly Junction
B = Tycoch Loop Junction

to Carmarthen

Incomplete earthworks
intended line to Van

FOUR ROADS

Four Roads

Quarry

Brickworks

GARREG

Y

MYNYDD

Stephens Silica
Brick Co.

Lime
works

MYNYDD Y GARREG

MINKIE ROAD

Kidwelly
Tin Plate
Works

Brickworks

Incomplete earthworks
of proposed "Coal Line"

Gwendraeth

Fach

KIDWELLY

Brickworks
/Saw mill

A

B

Brick
works

Gwendraeth

Burry   Port   &   Gwendreath   Valley   Railway

Carway
Colliery
Sidings

to Pontyberem

to Trimsaran

to Burry Port

to Burry Port

Kidwelly-Quay

to Carmarthen

Jde H 335

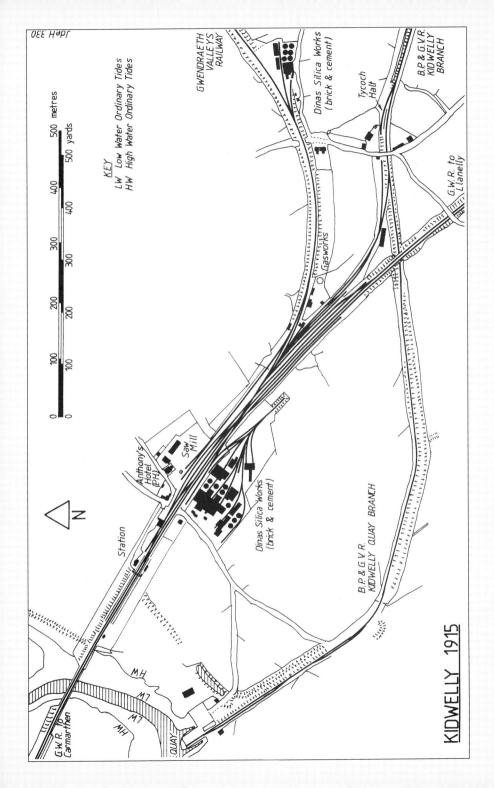

KIDWELLY 1915

Kidwelly station, looking west with Swindon-built 'Cross Country' dmu entering on a train from Swansea in August 1964. *Author*

Kidwelly station, looking east from the down platform. Note the water tank beyond the level crossing gates in this 1964 view. *R.E. Bowen*

Anthony's Hotel, Kidwelly, in the early years of this century. To the right, the sidings which originally served Edwards' Brickworks can be seen. *B. Cripps*

Kidwelly station and goods shed, as seen from the level crossing at th east end of the station - i.e. view looking west *c.* 1964. *R.E. Bowen Collection*

Stephens' Brickworks, Kidwelly, as seen from the level crossing east of Kidwelly station in 1964.
R.E. Bowen Collection

The GVR at Kidwelly on 24th July, 1960. Note the line to Mynydd-y-Garreg curving away to the left and the line to the BP&GVR at Tycoch to the right. The fencing marks the limit of GWR property.   *M. Hale*

'coal line' of the 1860s; by the Edwardian period a second shorter siding had been provided just to the south. The earthworks of the old 'coal line' remained in place until 1943, when they were removed to provide additional spoil for an extension to Pembrey airfield.

To describe the Mynydd-y-Garreg line as the GVR's 'main line' may seem to imply an importance and a volume of traffic that this route never knew! However, the GVR perceived it as such, even though it consisted of only a single track climbing across the fields north of Kidwelly. Half a mile from the junction the line ran through a deep cutting, passing under a stone-built bridge carrying Monksford Street, on the edge of Kidwelly. Swinging to the north-east it then passed a couple of fields east of Llangadog Farm after three-quarters of a mile, before coming alongside an old cart track on the way to Waungadog Farm, just over a mile from the junction. Just before the farm there was an ungated crossing over a quiet country lane; directly opposite the farm, on the east side of the line, there was for many years a water tank. It is believed that this was intended primarily for farm use, but according to local folk lore it was quite common for the locomotive to stop at Waungadog to replenish its own tanks. Whatever the truth of the matter, a short run brought trains to the level crossing over the road from Kidwelly to Four Roads, and the nearby village of Meinciau. The crossing was protected by boards instructing enginemen to sound the whistle, and gates about 6 ft tall of a rather unusual fence like design, effectively guarding road users during those occasions when the locomotive was shunting across the Meinciau road. As Englishmen at Paddington could not cope with this piece of Welsh spelling and pronunciation, the GWR named this spot Minkie Road; local people always referred to it as 'the Sidings'.

In spite of its local name, there were few sidings at Minkie Road (1¾ miles from Kidwelly). A loop siding on the east side served the loading wharf used by Stephens' Silica Brick Co. Ltd for transporting stone and sand from their Mynydd-y-Garreg quarries. On the north-west side of the line, another loop siding was provided for coal and other wagon-load traffic. A black timber-built platelayers' hut here was known as 'Shed ddu'; the small brick office and weighbridge building was sometimes described as 'shed goch'. Just beyond the boundary of railway land to the west was situated Mynydd-y-Garreg's little church, dedicated to St Teilo and opened in 1892.

Just north of 'the Sidings' the track divided, the eastern branch bridging a minor road at Shintor before following the original Carmarthen & Cardigan alignment to the top of the lime kilns and Alexander Young's line to Penymynydd, Four Roads. On one occasion in the 1920s it is said that a GWR driver named Lewis saw in the distance a runaway wagon heading down this line towards him. Acting on the assumption that it should be stopped as quickly as possible, he apparently took his engine forward to meet it, thereby risking derailment and injury. In the event he and his locomotive emerged unscathed, although the same could not be said for the wagon! In later years the stub of this line was sometimes referred to as 'the mileage siding'. The other branch dropped towards a level crossing over the same minor road before passing the base of the 1872 lime kilns to terminate at two sidings on the edge of the nearby fields. This was the official terminus of the GVR, known for many

The overbridge carrying the B4308 road over the route of the former Gwendraeth Valley Railway at Kidwelly, 31st May, 1991.   *Author*

The line looking down past Waungadog crossing, between Mynydd-y-Garreg and Kidwelly.
                                                                          Author

Above: The course of the GVR at Llangadog, south of Minkie Road, 31st May, 1991.
Author

Left: The loading bank at Minkie Road, 31st May, 1991.
Author

Right: The empty expanse left at the abandoned site of the Gwendraeth Valleys Railway between 'The Sidings' and Mynydd-y-Garreg, 2nd March, 1990.
Author

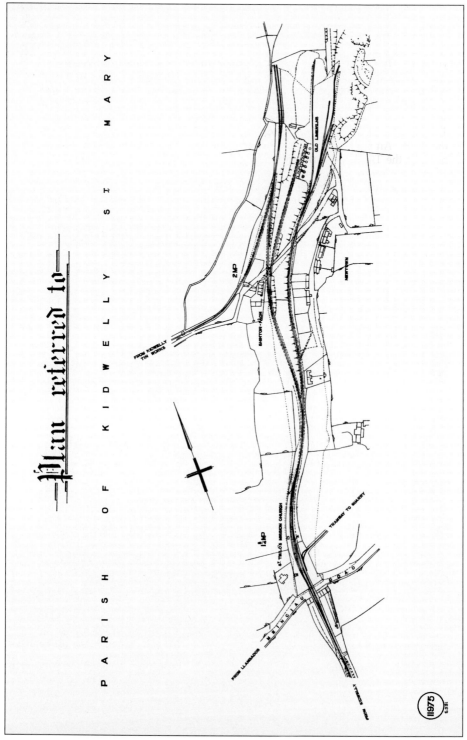

Plan referred to

PARISH OF KIDWELLY St MARY

FROM KIDWELLY TIN WORKS

OLD LLANELLY

2 MP

BANTOR-VACH

NEWTOWN

TRAMWAY TO QUARRY

ST TEILO'S MISSION CHURCH

1⅜ MP

KEINCAU ROAD

FROM LLANELLY

FROM KIDWELLY

11975
6.331

British Railways

An undated track plan of Mynydd-y-Garreg.

years as Mynydd-y-Garreg goods depot, 2 miles 14 chains from Kidwelly. Apart from an old van body and a small building, perhaps an office or a tiny cottage, situated between the limekilns and the sidings below, there is no evidence of any covered accommodation being built. Instead the two sidings seem to have been used simply to hold wagons to and from the Kidwelly Tinplate Works, reached by another siding running back across the fields from the GVR. An OS map dated 1912 shows another small structure right on the route of the Tinplate Works siding, which was quite possibly a weighbridge. Within the works there were two sidings down the east side of the main premises, a small brick-built engine shed to the north, and several other sidings on the west, one of which extended to the southern boundary of the site. Over the whole length of the GVR there were only three bridges (one over, and two under) and no rail-served building larger than the Kidwelly locomotive shed. Surely no public railway company in the British Isles ever had fewer structures to maintain!

Mynydd-y-Garreg, 1973. The site of Threlfall's huge limekilns is concealed behind the bushes, bottom right. The alignment of the railway spur to the tinworks can be seen cutting across the fields on the right. Kidwelly Castle and parish church can be seen in the distance, with the Burry Inlet beyond.   *Llanelli Public Library*

Coed Bach washery on 3rd March, 1973. Class '03' diesel shunters Nos. 2142 and 2145 work back to back.   *Author*

'03' class shunters Nos. 2142 and 2145 on the headshunt south-west of Coed Bach washery, on the former BP&GVR Kidwelly branch, on 3rd March, 1973. So far as is known British Railways never sent a diesel over the Gwendraeth Valleys line to Mynydd-y-Garreg - but this class of diesel did work almost to Tycoch, if only to marshall wagons for storage.   *Author*

Chapter Eleven

Postscript

The closure and dismantling of the Gwendraeth Valleys line in the 1960s was not quite the end of the story. In 1953 the NCB had opened a coal washery at Coed Bach, about 1½ miles north-east of Kidwelly, near Kidwelly Junction on the former BP&GV line. Following the closure of Tycoch Junction the only access to Coed Bach was from the BP&GV route, although most of the track south to Tycoch remained in place for many years and was used for wagon storage. Meanwhile the restricted clearances on the BP&GV line meant that after the demise of the '16XX' class 0-6-0 pannier tanks in 1965 traffic could only be worked by a handful of '03' class diesel shunters, suitably modified. Just as two or three pannier tanks might be required to work heavy trains, so two or three of these '03' diesels might be used on a single train - a labour intensive arrangement.

In due course these diesels became weary, but as the route continued to offer coal traffic - mostly from open-cast mines - British Rail had to take some decisions for the future. The major decision was one which might have been taken quite reasonably years earlier. This was to rebuild the railway between the South Wales main line at Kidwelly and Coed Bach washery, with clearances sufficient for heavy coal trains. Parliamentary powers were obtained for this purpose in 1982, incidentally providing legislative authority for the first time for the former GVR section from the main line to Tycoch. The reinstated track was actually laid slightly closer to the main line over much of this distance, but the remainder to Coed Bach followed the BP&GV alignment after some very necessary engineering works had been undertaken to improve drainage. The cost of these works amounted to £1.2 million - a sum almost unimaginable to either the GVR or the BP&GVR of earlier years.

The completion of these works was soon followed by the closure of the BP&GV between Burry Port and Kidwelly Junction, near Coed Bach, with effect from 17th September, 1983.

All traffic was now routed by the restored line from Kidwelly, and main line diesels - usually the English Electric class '37' locomotives - were allowed to work up the line as far as Coed Bach. In this way the short resuscitated section of the GVR came to carry engines far heavier than anything seen in its independent era. Meanwhile, as the class '03' shunters became due for retirement, another decision was taken regarding motive power. In 1985 one of the '08' 350 hp 0-6-0 diesel shunters was given a cut-down cab and body and dispatched to Landore for trials on the BP&GV. These were deemed a success, and in 1986 two more '08s' were similarly converted, and the last of the Gwendraeth Valley '03s' was withdrawn soon after. In the 1990s traffic diminished, and the BP&GVR north of Coed Bach was closed with effect from 29th March, 1996. At the time of writing in August 1997, the track remains, but the closure of the Coed Bach washery is forecast. If this occurs it will surely serve to close the remainder of the BP&GVR.

The site of Tycoch Halt (to the left of the milepost) on the relaid line from Kidwelly to Coed Bach washery, 8th July, 1993. *Author*

Class '37' diesel running light to Coed Bach washery from Kidwelly and photographed just north of Tycoch Halt on the 8th July, 1993. *Author*

Class '37' No. 37 703 pulls away from the run-round loop at Kidwelly with a train of coal from Coed Bach washery for Immingham, 8th July, 1993. *Author*

Kidwelly, view looking east on 8th July, 1993. the land to the left was the site of the GVR tracks, the locomotive shed being located formerly by the site of the bungalow, and the route to Mynydd-y-Garreg to the extreme left. The run-round loop for trains to and from Coed Bach is in the middle of the picture, and across the main line, to the extreme right the bushes mark the site of the former siding access into Stephens' Brickworks, Kidwelly. *Author*

The story of the Mynydd-y-Garreg route of the GVR has been quite different. Between the main line junction and the site of the demolished bridge over the main road in Kidwelly much of the land is privately owned, part of it being a garden to a sizeable bungalow built on the trackbed in 1968. North of the main road a footpath skirts the old Smart's brickworks site, now in other commercial hands. After passing through the cutting below the road to Trimsaran, the footpath ends at the Kidwelly by-pass (opened 1994) where it cuts across the GVR just south of Waungadog Farm. From a small country lane to the north of Waungadog the trackbed is again used as a footpath up to the site of 'the Sidings' at Minkie Road. Here the wall of the stone loading wharf can be seen. but little else. There is scant sign of what are thought to have been Owen Bowen's quarries and kilns, as the area has been subject to infilling, new building, or neglect. The site of Threlfall's huge kilns is now but a steep overgrown bank, whilst the location of the sidings marking the terminus of the GVR has also returned to nature. Although the old tinplate works is now the Kidwelly Industrial Museum, most of the route of the railway serving the site has been taken back into the fields from which it was cut.

The other industrial locations formerly served by the GVR do not present any better picture. The lower part of the incline from Minkie Road up to Stephens' quarry is heavily overgrown, whilst the section in cutting higher up has been partially filled with rubbish. Parts of the quarries are inaccessible, but the lower level 'The Deep' has flooded to form a small lake in the middle of the workings. One or two buildings still stand near the site of the Llyn quarry, but these only add to the air of desolation. At Young's brickworks may be seen the ruined base of a stone crusher and the rubble of perhaps three kilns. At Penymynydd the ivy-clad limekilns still possess a certain dignity, whilst Young's engine shed has since 1978 found a new function as a small milking parlour for the cattle on the farm. After such a long and chequered history it is surely ironic that the only significant railway structures in existence are this converted industrial engine shed, and the fine broad gauge bridge at Gledwyn which never carried a train at all! The Gwendraeth Valleys Railway has gone, but at these sites north of Mynydd-y-Garreg it is still possible to get a glimpse of what it was all about.

Kidwelly Industrial Museum on 25th June, 1990. Peckett 0-6-0ST 2114 of 1951 stands near the headgear from Morlais. *Author*

204 hp diesel mechanical locomotive built by Andrew Barclay (393 of 1954), formerly employed at Carmarthen Bay Power Station, at Kidwelly Industrial Museum on the site of Kidwelly Tinplate Works, 25th June, 1990. *Author*

The Kidwelly Tinplate Works seen from the north on 8th July, 1993. The colliery headframe to the right was moved to the site from Morlais Colliery, Llangennech, to enable the Kidwelly Industrial Museum, now established at this location, to include this coal mining exhibit. *Author*

Appendix One

Working Agreement Between GVR and BP&GVR, November 1876

ARTICLES OF AGREEMENT made the Thirtieth day of November One Thousand Eight hundred and Seventy-six between the GWENDRAETH VALLEYS RAILWAY COMPANY (who and their successors and assigns are hereinafter called the Gwendraeth Valleys Company) of the one part and The BURRY PORT and GWENDRAETH VALLEY RAILWAY COMPANY (who and their successors and assigns are hereinafter called 'The Burry Port Company') of the other part.

WHEREAS the Gwendraeth Valleys Company are the Owners of the Line of Railway from Mynyddygarreg in the County of Carmarthen to a Junction with the Great Western Railway at Kidwelly and with a Branch to Tycoch And whereas by an Agreement dated the Twenty-eighth day of February One thousand Eight hundred and Seventy-six made between the parties hereto certain arrangements were made as to traffic and otherwise And whereas the Burry Port Company are the owners of a Line of Railway extending from Pontyberem to Burry Port with various branches and amongst others a Branch from a certain place called Spudders Bridge Junction to Tycoch and to Kidwelly Quay And whereas it is desirable for the convenience of the parties hereto that other arrangements should be made for the working of the traffic between Spudders Bridge Tycoch Junction and Kidwelly Quay as well as for traffic arising on the Gwendraeth Valleys Company or any of such places and that the said Agreement of the Twenty-eighth day of February One thousand Eight hundred and Seventy-six shall remain in abeyance as hereinafter provided And whereas the parties hereto are desirous of entering into this Agreement for the purpose of better carrying out such other arrangements and more effectually working the said traffic It is hereby agreed by and between the parties hereto as follows that is to say:

1. There shall be at all times a union between the Gwendraeth Valleys Railway and the Bury Port Railway at Tycoch.
2. The Burry Port Company shall at their own cost find and provide and work and run an engine once or twice a day or oftener if the traffic should require it for the purpose of taking the traffic from their Railway to and over the junction called Tycoch Junction with the said Gwendraeth Valleys Railway and also to and from the Kidwelly Junction of the Great Western Railway to Mynyddygarreg Lime Works and effectually work the traffic of the Gwendraeth Valleys Company to and from and over both the said junctions and to and from the said Lime Works under the direction of the traffic manager of the Gwendraeth Valleys Company in conjunction with the manager of the Burry Port Company and in case they should not agree it shall be referred to the district traffic manager of the Great Western Railway Company for the time being to decide and settle all matters in difference and direct and order what course shall be taken when any such disputes shall arise and his decision and direction shall be final and conclusive between the parties.
3. The traffic rates and tolls set out in the First Schedule hereunder written shall he the minimum rates and tolls to be collected and received by the Gwendraeth Valleys Company and shall be collected and received by such Company and out of the said rates and tolls there shall be allowed to them the said Gwendraeth Valleys Company One hundred pounds per annum as remuneration for such collection and the arrangement and consignment of the traffic by them.

4. The Gwendraeth Valleys Company shall be credited with and shall receive Sixpence per ton on all traffic which arises on the Burry Port Company's Railway North of Spudders Bridge and consigned and sent in a westerly direction whether such traffic shall be taken by way of Burry Port or Tycoch Junction.

5. The Gwendraeth Valleys Company shall furnish a monthly statement of all traffic over their line to the Burry Port Company and they the said Burry Port Company will furnish a statement to the Gwendraeth Valleys Company of all the traffic conveyed and sent in a westerly direction as aforesaid.

6. The Gwendraeth Valleys Company shall upon notice from the Burry Port Company from time to time maintain and keep in good and sufficient order and repair and renew when necessary the permanent way fences engines house and accommodation works of the Gwendraeth Valleys Company from the said Junction with the Great Western Railway to Tycoch Junction aforesaid and also to the said Lime Works at Mynyddygarreg and of all sidings and any extension of their said Railway and sidings. In case the Gwendraeth Valleys Company make default in so maintaining and repairing the permanent way and works immediately after such notice the Burry Port Company may execute such repairs and deduct the cost thereof from any tonnages and tolls payable by them to the Gwendraeth Valleys Company under this Agreement and if any disagreement shall arise between the parties hereto as to the maintenance or whether the repairs executed by the Burry Port Company are necessary and proper the question in difference shall be referred to the local engineer of the Great Western Railway Company for the time being who shall decide the same.

7. The accounts shall be made up on the Thirty-first day of March the Thirtieth day of June the Thirtieth day of September and the Thirty-first day of December in every year and the amount found to be due to or from either Company ascertained as near as can be but in any case the Burry Port Company shall be paid not less then One hundred and Fifty pounds quarterly either by means of the per centage secured to them by this Agreement and a payment in cash by the Gwendraeth Valleys Company or by either of those means.

8. A settlement of accounts shall be come to between the parties hereto half-yearly on the Thirtieth day of June and the Thirty-first day of December in every year and the amount found at such dates to be due to either Company from the other shall be paid within One calendar month.

9. That the services required of the Burry Port Company in working the traffic as aforesaid shall consist of hauling and shunting the traffic and doing other things incident thereto and usually done in such cases to the reasonable satisfaction of the traders and in accordance with the spirit of this Agreement and the remuneration of the Burry Port Company for such said services shall be as follows that is to say when the amount of the gross traffic inclusive of the aforesaid sum of One hundred pounds and the amount that may be placed to the credit of the Gwendraeth Valleys Company pursuant to Clause 4 is more than One thousand Six hundred pounds in any one year they shall receive from and the Gwendraeth Valleys Company shall pay them Forty pounds per cent. on such amount but whatever may be the amount of gross traffic that they shall in no year receive a less remuneration than the sum of Six hundred pounds and the same rate of Forty pounds per cent. shall apply to any increase of traffic caused by the extension of any old or new works of collieries on or near either to the said Gwendraeth Valleys Railway or Burry Port Railway respectively and the tolls collectable shall be in accordance with the said First Schedule hereunder written and also to any increase arising from the next succeeding clause.

10. The tolls and charges set out in the Second Schedule hereunder written shall be the maximum tolls and charges of the Burry Port Company on all traffic to Tycoch Junction or other places therein mentioned and such tolls and charges shall not be increased in anyway whatsoever without the consent in writing of the Gwendraeth Valleys Company but if so increased by arrangement of the parties it is expressly agreed that the Gwendraeth Valleys Company shall be entitled to receive one equal moiety of the proceeds of such said increase which shall he carried to the general account of the Gwendraeth Valleys Company of which the Burry Port Company are to receive Forty pounds per cent.

11. The Gwendraeth Valleys Company shall provide all water required for engines of the Burry Port Company in working the traffic as aforesaid the Kidwelly water rate if any to be paid by the Burry Port Company.

12. The Gwendraeth Valleys Company to put down an extra siding adjoining the Great Western Railway sufficient for the traffic within Three months from the date hereof.

13. The engine-house at Kidwelly may be used by the Burry Port Company during the existence of this Agreement but it shall always be and remain the property of the Gwendraeth Valleys Company and be given up to them on the termination of this Agreement.

14. In case the remuneration received by the Burry Port Company under this Agreement shall be less in any year than Six hundred pounds the Burry Port Company shall have the option by giving Three months' notice in writing to the Gwendraeth Valleys Company under the Seal of their Company to be delivered or left at the offices of the Gwendraeth Valleys Company of their intention so to do to determine this Agreement and unless the said sum of Six hundred pounds he paid or made up on or before the expiration of the said Three months then this Agreement shall on the expiration of the said Three months cease and be void but without prejudice to any existing rights or claims of either Company at the date of such termination.

15. That this Agreement (save as to Clause 1) which shall be binding on the parties hereto their successors and assigns in perpetuity shall remain in force and be effectual for the term of Ten years from the date hereof until the same shall be determined under the preceding Clause and the said Agreement of the Twenty-eighth day of February One Thousand Eight hundred and Seventy-six shall be and remain in abeyance and be of no force and effect during the continuance of this Agreement but if from any cause whatsoever this Agreement shall become inoperative or void or shall cease then the said Agreement of the Twenty-eighth day of February One Thousand Eight hundred and Seventy-six shall revive and become of full force and virtue for the then remainder of the term therein mentioned as if these presents had not been made but without prejudice to any then existing rights of either Company.

16. These Articles of Agreement are subject to the sanction of Parliament and to such alterations as Parliament may think proper to make therein. In witness whereof the said Companies have hereunto caused their respective Common Seals to be affixed the day and year first above written.

THE FIRST SCHEDULE ABOVE REFERRED TO

The GWENDRAETH VALLEYS COMPANY'S TOLLS and CHARGES to and from the undermentioned Places.

To and From	Great Western	Tycoch Junction	For Shipment Tycoch Junction	Level Crossing	Mynyddy-garreg
	d.	d.	d.	d.	d.
Mynyddygarreg Limestone and other Traffic	7	7	6	3	-
Level Crossing	6	6	6	-	3
Harris and Redford	6	6	6	6	7
Kidwelly Brick Works	4	6	6	6	7
Great Western	-	6	6	6	7
Coal Yard at Tycoch	6	4	4	6	7

Any charges levied by the Gwendraeth Valleys Company for terminals sidings accommodation and all other charges belonging to the working of the above traffic shall be divided in the same manner as the above tolls and charges.

THE SECOND SCHEDULE ABOVE REFERRED TO

The BURRY PORT COMPANY'S MAXIMUM TOLLS and CHARGES

To and from the different collieries to Tycoch Junction One penny half-penny per Ton per mile with Three pence per Ton added for siding accommodation at the collieries weighing and collections of traffic therefrom.

To and from Kidwelly Quay to Tycoch Junction Three pence per Ton.

To and from the Burry Port Docks for shipment to Tycoch Junction for sand lime bricks One Shilling and Two pence per Ton.

To and from Pembrey (or Burry Port) to Tycoch Junction for sand lime bricks One shilling per Ton.

The Common Seal of the Gwendraeth Valleys)   The
Railway Company was affixed in the presence of)   Common Seal of
                                                    the Gwendraeth
    JOHN HALL   )   Directors   Valleys Railway
    CHARLES LINGS   )   Company

    S.W. WILLIAMSON,   Secretary   The
                                                   Common Seal of
                                                 The Burry Port and
                                                     Gwendraeth
                                                   Valley Railway
                                                      Company

Appendix Two

Letter of John Russell, BP&GVR, 1898

Concerning Possible Purchase of GVR, 1898

All communications to be addressed to the Company
The Burry Port & Gwendraeth Valley
Railway Company
Burry Port, R.S.C. South Wales

30th June, 1898

Dear Mr Herring,

In compliance with my promise to Mr Williamson to bring his desire to sell the Gwendraeth Valleys line before those who were backing up this Company, I send you his letters and my answers, you will see that he does not notice my enquiry whether the Bondholders would be disposed to part with the Junction line between Tycoch and the Great Western, which was *not* constructed, I have been told, and believe, out of the Capital raised under the Gwendraeth Valleys Railway Act - it we could get the Junction line only, on easy terms, it would be good business, for then the relaying of the Kidwelly Branch (about 2 miles) would not be like throwing money away, for direct access by our own line to the Great Western at Kidwelly would be a grand thing. As it is now, all traffic via Tycoch pays the Valleys Company 4*d*. a Ton, consequently the West traffic is strangled, if we got the Junction line the 4*d*. charge would cease and be a mileage charge (the Junction line is less than 500 yards) if the Tinplate Works were re opened, no loss on their traffic to the Gwendraeth Valleys Company would follow, as the 4*d*. rate would be the rate to the Junction, or Great Western, as now it is so with their other Trader, the Lime Works Company.

I send you a tracing showing the Junction line, and the Carmarthen & Cardigan Railway (Kidwelly Branch) Act 1864.

Under Agreement we hire to the Valleys Company a Loco at £40 per cent on their gross Income, to enable them to work their traffic, with 3 months notice on either side - since the Tin Works closed I arranged that we should work their traffic as we do other traffic, and the Agreement should be in suspense till the Tin Works re opened, continuing to receive £40 per cent as hire, this I thought better than giving notice to terminate the Agreement, as I did it would probably shut up the line, or they might worry this Company over accommodation sidings at Tycoch Junction. The Loco was at the disposal of the Manager all day.

If you think that negotiations to purchase the Junction line worth consideration, but that the Valleys line proper is not worth having as a Gift, I would on hearing from you write accordingly to Mr Williamson - the Receiver -

Yours truly

John Russell

George Herring Esqr.
1 Hamilton Place

P.S. This offer to sell is by no means the first.

Appendix Three

Reports and GWR Correspondence Concerning the GVR, 1922

THE GWENDRAETH VALLEY RAILWAY COMPANY

Quite a separate undertaking from the Burry Port & Gwendraeth Valley Railway.

Length etc.,
The line which is a single one is only three miles long. It is connected with the GWR and the BP&GVR, at Kidwelly and extends to Mynyddgarreg.

History and Capital
The Gwendraeth Valley Railway Company was incorporated by an Act dated 28th April, 1864 - other Acts 1865 and 1866 - to take over the Kidwelly extension of the Carmarthen and Cardigan Railway. Authorised Capital £170,000, Debentures Loans permitted £56,000.

From 1886 to 1905 the Railway was, apparently, worked by the Burry Port and Gwendraeth Valley Co. but from 1906 onwards the line has been worked by the Gwendraeth Valley Railway Co.'s own engines.

In 1892 the Chairman and Secretary were appointed by the Court of Chancery to be Receivers and Managers, and as years went on the Secretary apparently became sole Receiver, and was discharged by the Court of Chancery in 1905.

According to the Gwendraeth Valley Railway Co.'s statement of accounts for 1914 the Capital is shown as £100,000 with £33,300 Debentures. This, however, cannot be accepted as indicating the Capital of the concern at the present time. When the Receiver was discharged in 1905, the new Company paid him £3,000 for the whole of the ordinary Capital and the Debentures issued by the Company.

At this period of the Gwendraeth Valley Company did not possess any Engines or Rolling stock so that the amount of £3,000 was only in respect of the land and a very indifferent Permanent Way.

Description of Line
The line is used for Goods Traffic only, has never been used for passenger traffic, and is not signalled. Traffic is worked as required up and down the line without a brakevan.

Rolling Stock Owned
The Gwendraeth Valley Railway Company possesses two small tank engines, 19 small open wagons, and 10 covered vans, but none of their goods vehicles appear to work on to other Companies' lines.

Industries Served
The only industries directly served by the Gwendraeth Valley Railway are:

A.Y. Dinas Silica Works
Kidwelly Tinplate Works
Silica Stone Quarries
Smart's Silica Brick Works

and the line depends mainly upon these industries for its existence.

In addition there are two coal sidings on the Gwendraeth Valley Railway property at Kidwelly and a private siding serving the small local Gas Works.

Traffic

According to the Gwendraeth Valley Railway Co.'s record the tonnage of traffic *originating on their line* during 1913 and 1916 was as under:

1913	54,378 tons
1916	52,550 tons

In addition to traffic arising on the Gwendraeth Valley Railway there are about 80 trucks of coal per month from the Burry Port and Gwendraeth Valley Line Collieries handed to us at Kidwelly via the GV Co.'s Junction at Tycoch for West Wales.

The total exchange between the GWR and the GVR at Kidwelly amounts to, approximately 48,000 tons per annum, and if to this is added traffic which is 'domestic' to the GV Rly, to the extent of about 40,000 tons per annum, an approximate idea of the total tonnage handled would be obtained.

The 'domestic' traffic consists principally of Silica Stone traffic from the Quarry at Mynyddgarreg for Messrs Smart and Co.'s and Messrs Stephens' Brickworks. Other 'domestic' traffic consists of coal from the BP&GVR, to the Works etc., on the Gwendraeth Valley Railway.

Charges

All inwards traffic arriving ex the GW line for the GVR, is invoiced to Kidwelly, and in a similar way all Outwards traffic handed us by the Gwendraeth Valley Railway is entered up from Kidwelly GWR at the Kidwelly rates.

The Gwendraeth Valley Company collect their own charges, the rates being

for Stone traffic ex the Quarry to Brickworks	10*d*. per ton
for other traffic	1*s*. per ton

The stone traffic from the Quarry for Messrs Stephens & Co.'s Brick Works - which are situated on the down side of the GW line - has to be lifted by us across our main lines and placed into the firm's private siding, for which we receive 2*s*. per wagon (i.e. 1*s*. plus 100%).

Allowance formerly made to GVR, by GWR

The Line has never been in a flourishing state, and in consequence of representations made to the GWR in 1877 an Allowance was made by the GWR to the GVR, upon the traffic handed to and received from the GVR. This was done in consequence of the bankrupt position of the undertaking and in order to keep the line open. The Allowance was at the rate of 2*d*. or 1*d*. per ton, according to traffic. This allowance continued to be made up to the end of 1908. Notice was given during 1908 that the Allowance would cease at the close of that year, but as a result of an urgent appeal it was continued year by year until the end of 1914, after which the GWR declined to continue it.

In respect of the year 1914 this rebate amounted to £300 15*s*. 8*d*., and this was paid upon a tonnage (estimated) of 45,059 tons, with a rail value of £7,880.

Condition of line and property

The following brief notes will give an idea as to the condition of the Permanent Way, etc.,

Permanent Way

This is overgrown with weeds. In places sleepers are comparatively new, but generally in bad condition, and the track, which consists of a light flanged rail secured by bolts to the sleepers, needs relaying and re-sleepering. The fence is in poor condition and needs repair generally.

Gradients and Curves

There is a gradual rise from the Kidwelly end which becomes rather severe approaching the connection to the Tinplate Works and beyond. The ruling gradient would be 1 in 40, but there are no very sharp curves.

Water Supply

Water for engines is obtained at Kidwelly and at the Tinplate Works.

Possible Economies

When the coal trade is normal, in addition to the coal for West Wales handed to us at Kidwelly, there is a regular flow of coal traffic for the GW stations in the same District handed to us by the BP&GVR at *Pembrey*, amounting approximately to 14,000 tons per annum.

If both the BP&GVR, and the Gwendraeth Valley Railway are acquired by the GWR it would be more economical for *all* the coal traffic for Kidwelly and west thereof arising on the BP&GV Line to come to the GW Line at Kidwelly, thus saving haulage to the extent of about seven miles on each wagon, i.e.:

Pembrey to Kidwelly, GW	5 miles
Saving on BP&GVR, to Kidwelly as against Burry Port	2 miles

In addition we should also obtain much desired relief at Pembrey in the handling of exchange traffic as the work of separating the Up and Down line coal traffic would be obviated.

Regarding staff economies the existing small operating and permanent way staff could not be reduced but the headquarters staff consisting of:

Manager
Accountant
Junior Clerk

could be dispensed with.

****

RAILWAYS ACT, 1921.

Gwendraeth Valleys Railway Company.

Notes of Meeting held at Paddington on May 25th 1922.

PRESENT:

Mr Pole	Mr D. Williams
Mr Bolter	Mr J. Thomas
Mr Hubbard	Mr M. Richards
	Mr H.E. Smart

Mr Thomas explained the circumstances under which the Kidwelly Tinplate Company had in 1905 purchased from the Receiver of the Gwendraeth Valleys Railway the whole of the Loans and Ordinary Shares of the Company for a sum of £3,000 and that these were now held by nominees of the Tinplate Company.

A discussion ensued as to the financial position of the Gwendraeth Valleys Company as disclosed by the published Accounts for 1921, Mr Pole pointing out that for this year there had been a net loss amounting to £3,855 on the working and that the total debit balance stood at £55,727. He said that it appeared from a report before him that the permanent way and fences were in a very poor condition, and enquired whether the present owners would accept what they paid for the undertaking, viz, £3,000.

Mr Richards replied that such an offer could not be accepted and, while declining to make any counter proposals, said that the year 1921 was no fair criterion of the operations of the railway, as for nine months the Kidwelly Tinplate Works, the chief source of traffic, had been closed down. In 1920, a small net profit had been secured. He explained, however, that when the Tinplate Company in 1905 acquired the line this had not been done with the idea of securing a profit from the working, but in order to obtain adequate railway facilities for their works which were not then available.

The representatives of the Gwendraeth Company expressed surprise at the report referred to by Mr Pole as to the state of maintenance of the railway. It was stated that since 1905 over three-fourths of the track had been re-laid, involving very considerable expenditure and in respect of which some consideration in the terms of purchase was expected. It was claimed that the line was in very fair condition.

It was intended on behalf of the Great Western Company that in view of the financial position of the undertaking, it was not possible to find justification for suggesting any more generous terms for its purchase than those named, and in these circumstances suggested that inquiry be held locally so that an estimate might be formed of the value of the railway to the Great Western Company as affording access to the Kidwelly Tinplate and other works in the locality. This proposal was agreed to and Mr Pole undertook to arrange for the District Goods Manager at Swansea to convene a meeting with representatives of the Gwendraeth Company.

****

> Great Western Railway,
> Divisional Engineer's Office,
> Neath.
> 14th June, 1922

Dear Sir,

Gwendraeth Valley Railway

There are no plans of any material value available except the 1/2500 Ordnance Survey, and I am accordingly sending you three sheets shewing by pink colouring the Gwendraeth Valley Railway Company's taking so far as I have been able to ascertain it from the Company's Manager, Mr Smart.

The line was constructed under an Act of Parliament in 1863, as part of the Kidwelly Branch of the Carmarthen and Cardigan Junction Railway. It was completed about 1872. Its length, from the Junction with the GWR at Kidwelly to Mynydd-y-gareg, is 2 m. 15½ chns. There is no system of signalling and no telegraph or telephone, and the line is worked as a siding.

Gradients The original gradient section shewn on the deposited plans has not been worked to beyond 0 m. 60 chns. and it will be necessary to have a longitudinal section made if it is considered requisite.

Bridges There are two Underbridges and one Overbridge.

No. 1   Underbridge at 0 m. 24¼ chns. - Stone abutments and parapets, brick arch - span
         24 ft 6 in. - width 32 ft 0 in. width between parapets 29 ft 0 in. In good condition.

No. 2   Overbridge at 0 m. 52¾ chns. - Stone Abutments and parapets, brick arch - span
         29 ft 0 in. on square, 30 ft 0 in. on skew. In good condition.

No. 3   Underbridge at 2 m. 23 chns. - stone abutments and pilasters, timber hand-rail. 4
         rolled steel joists and 4 in. timber decking. All in good condition except decking
         which requires renewal.

Fencing This is all post and wire, the spacing of posts varying from about 6 ft to 9 ft, and
the number of wires from 4 to 7, with the top wire generally barbed. The posts are
roughly cut, mostly from small trees, and the fencing generally would require a good deal
of attention and renewal.

Level Crossings There are two Public Road Level Crossings.
No. 1 at 1 m. 57½ chns. Meinciau Road, carrying 2 lines with 20 ft checks. Gates are fixed
but they are chained back and not used. They are in poor condition.
No. 2 at 2 m. 1 chn. carrying two lines. No checks provided and no gates.

There are 12 Occupation Level Crossings with, generally speaking, iron gates. 4 New
gates required.

Loco. Sheds There is a small Engine Shed at Kidwelly 38 ft x 17½ ft of brick and slates, in
fair condition. There are two Locomotives - 6-wheel coupled - weight about 35 tons.

Truck Weighbridges There is a 50 ton truck weighbridge at Kidwelly (0 m. 7 c.) with 17 ft
table in good condition, also a weighbridge house 32 ft x 14 ft of brick and slates in fair
condition. It is divided into two rooms - Manager's office and weigh-office.

Cart Weighbridges There are two cart weighbridges, one at Kidwelly and one at Meinciau
Road, each 12 ft x 6 ft with weighhouses of brick and slate - one 12¼ ft x 10½ ft at Kidwelly
and the other 12 ft x 8½ ft. They are both in good condition.

House Property One 4 room cottage at Meinciau Road, occupied by Engine Driver. Stone
and slate.

Permanent Way The Permanent Way is of flange rail on 9 ft x 10 ft x 5 in. sleepers
throughout, the weight of rails varying from about 60 to 75 lbs. As already stated the
length of running line is 2m. 15½ chns. The total length of sidings, including Junctions, is
about 2m. 8 chns. made up as follows.

84 chns. at Kidwelly Station with 11 Junctions and 1 three-throw
18 "   " Meinciau Road   "   4   "
66 "   " Mynydd-y-gareg   "   7   "

    About ½ mile of the running line is of 65 lb. flange rail, and the remainder of 75 lb.
flange rail. About 110 chains of siding is of 60 to 65 lb. flange rail and the remainder of
75 lb. Section. A 4 hole bracket and slip fastening is in use on about 40 chains of the

running line, but this was to have been done away with when renewals were carried out. About 1 mile of the running line has been patched, viz., 75 lb. rails of lengths varying from 26 ft to 40 ft with 9 to 17 sleepers respectively. New 36 ft and 40 ft rails have been used latterly in renewal. When relaying, only the worst sleepers have been removed and new ones, 9 ft x 10 ft x 5 in. substituted. The method of securing the rails to the sleeper is, in the more recent renewals, by dog-spike and fang at the joint and every alternate sleeper, and a dog-spike inside and outside to the other sleepers - two to every sleeper. There are 22 Junctions and 1 three-throw, with the exception of the Junction with the GWR Sidings of BH Section) and the three-throw (of 86A section). They are all of 60 to 75 lb. flange rail. 50 per cent require immediate renewal. There are, in addition, 3 private Junctions: 1 at Kidwelly to Gas Works and 2 at Tycoch - now disused.

Stop-blocks Nil.

Packers Huts There are 3 Huts, 10 ft x 8 ft timber, in fair condition.

Yours faithfully,

(signed) James Cunningham

W.W. Grierson, Esq.,

****

Great Western Railway,
Chief Goods Manager's Office,
Paddington Station,
London, W.2.

3rd July, 1922.

Dear Sir,

Railways Act, 1921 Gwendraeth Valleys Railway

Referring to your letter of May 26th; you will know that the late Mr Charles Roberts made a full report to you respecting this Railway during last year, and I would supplement the information then given you with the following particulars supplied by Mr James as a result of his inspection of the line.

The only industries directly served by the Gwendraeth Valleys Railway are:

Amalgamated Dinas Silica Works
Kidwelly Tinplate Works
Silica Stone Quarries
Smart's Silica Brick Works

The tonnage of the traffic *originating* on the line during 1913, 1917, 1918, 1919 and 1920 was as under:

Year	Tons
1913	54,378
1917	60,203
1918	49,401
1919	39,450
1920	48,101

This tonnage, however, does not represent the total tonnage passing over the line, and below I give you particulars of the total tonnages and receipts for 1918 and 1920:

Year	Traffic for and from	Tonnage	Rate per ton	Revenue derived from GV Co. charges
1918	Kidwelly Tinplate Co.	28,867	6d.	722
	Smart's & Stephens' Brickworks	36,797	5d.	767
	A.Y. Dinas Brickworks	8,987	6d.	225
	Other Traders*	3,387	6d.	85
	BP&GV Co.†	21,064	3d.	263
		99,102		2,062

Year	Traffic for and from	Tonnage	Rate per ton	Revenue derived from GV Co. charges
1920	Kidwelly Tinplate Co.	37,614	1s.	1,880
	Smart's & Stephens' Brickworks	33,456	10d.	1,394
	A.Y. Dinas Brickworks	8,744	11d.	401
	Other Traders*	4,916	6d.	123
	BP&GV Co.†	19,027	7d.	555
		103,757		4,353

*   Traffic for 'Other Traders' represents traffic dealt with at GV Co.'s coal yard at Kidwelly. Station, traffic loaded and unloaded at Minkie Siding, and that at Tycoch Coal Yard.

†   These figures represent traffic passing between BP&GVR and GVR and also to and from BP&GVR and GWR via GVR.

N.B.   Of the above tonnage, the following is approximately the proportion of traffic passing to and from GWR.

	1918	1920
Traffic excluding coal and Pitwood (see below)	36,540	50,740
Coal Traffic ex BP&GVR via GVR	9,740	9,255
Pitwood GWR to BP&GVR via GWR	5,590	8,046
	51,870	68,041

From these figures you will see that a substantial traffic passes to and from the GW Railway, a good proportion of the traffic received from the GVR being the valuable traffic from the Kidwelly Tinplate Works.

The Gwendraeth Valleys Company at present charge Local Tolls on all traffic passing over their line, whether originating on the line or from or for the GWR, but in the case of traffic passing to and from the BP&GV Railways the charges are collected by the BP&GV Company who allow the GV Company their Tolls.

The tolls were increased by approximately 100 per cent from 15th January, 1920. The tolls are fixed without regard to classification and no addition is made in respect of flat rates.

At the present time the Amalgamated Dinas Silica Works and their Quarries, and Smart's Silica Brick Works are idle in consequence to Trade depression, and it is not possible to say when operations will be resumed at these Works. There is no likelihood of any new industry being established upon the line, and beyond some development which may take place in connection with these Silica Brick Works and Quarries, I cannot find that there is any prospect of any increased traffic being put under the Gwendraeth Valleys Railway.

The possible economies, both working and staff, are set out in the late Mr Charles Robert's Report. The staff economies are not considerable, but the diversion of the whole of the West Wales Coal traffic from the Pembrey route to the Kidwelly route would afford much desired relief at Pembrey.

The Amalgamated Dinas Silica Works and Quarries, are situated upon a private line which connects with the Gwendraeth Valleys Railway at a point near its termination, and you will know that under your papers J.29.200, you are dealing with an application from the Amalgamated Dinas Silica Company regarding the acquisition of this private line by the Company.

The Engineer is reporting to you regarding the condition of the permanent way, fencing, etc.,

Yours truly,

(Signed) E. Lowther

F.J.C. Pole Esq.,
          Paddington.

****

RAILWAYS ACT, 1921.

GWENDRAETH VALLEYS RAILWAY.

Notes of Meeting held at Paddington on Wednesday,
1st November, 1922.

PRESENT:

Mr Pole   Mr J. Thomas
Mr Bolter   Mr H.E. Smart
Mr Cope   Mr Richards
Mr Hubbard

The General Manager referred to the discussion which took place on May 25th last when the offer made on behalf of the Great Western Company was stated to be unacceptable to the Gwendraeth's Company's Representatives, and he enquired whether they now had any alternative proposal to make.

Mr Richards stated that although it was a fact that the Kidwelly Tin-plate Company had, in 1905 purchased the whole of the loans and ordinary shares of the Gwendraeth Company for £3,000, a cash payment of this amount by the Great Western Company as the consideration to be paid for the undertaking was not considered to be a reasonable offer. He stated that the 1913 Accounts of the Gwendraeth Company did not indicate the true earning capacity of the line inasmuch as between the years 1905 and 1915 the rates charged on traffic to and from the Kidwelly Tin-plate Works had been on the basis of 4d. per ton instead of 6d., and no charge had been made for shunting and marshalling traffic by the railway engine at the Tin-plate works. The appropriate conveyance rate would have been 6d. per ton, and a charge of 6d. per ton should have been made for shunting and marshalling. Had charges on this latter basis been in operation for 1913, the net revenue would have been appreciated that year by an amount of about £2,500. Since January 1916 the conveyance rate had been 6d. per ton and was subject to the 100% increase in January 1920 and charges for shunting and marshalling had been in operation. He urged that this was a consideration which should be taken into account in arriving at the terms of absorption.

In reply Mr Pole referred to the provisions of the Railways Act which virtually stereotyped the net revenue of the group when formed to the aggregate net revenue for the year 1913 of the Constituent and Subsidiary Companies embraced therein, and stated that the basis of any arrangement arrived at must be that of the net revenue for the year 1913 of the undertaking as disclosed by the published accounts.

Doubt was expressed, as to whether the figure of £582 shown as the net receipts in 1913 had been properly arrived at in view of the fact that adequate provision had not been made for maintenance and renewal of permanent way and rolling stock. Further, it was questioned whether, even this level of net income was reasonably likely to be maintained. With a view, however, of effecting a settlement Mr Pole stated that the Great Western Company's offer might be increased to £10,000, the understanding being that this proposal was made entirely without prejudice, and would not be referred to in the event of reference to the Tribunal becoming necessary.

The Representatives of the Gwendraeth Company undertook to consider this offer, and arrangements were made for a further meeting to take place at 3.00 pm on Wednesday, November 8th.

Appendix Four

Mynydd-y-Garreg New Quarry
Hourly Pay Rates 1948/1949

	February 1948		February 1949	
	s.	d.	s.	d.
Labourers	2	1½	2	3
Banksmen	2	3¾	2	4¼
Brakesman	2	2¾	2	0¼
Haulier	2	2¼	2	3¾
Shunter	2	1½	2	3
Engine Driver (2s. per day lighting engine)	2	4½	2	6
Platelayer	2	2¼	2	4¾
Blacksmith	2	3½	2	5
Dumper Driver	2	3½	2	5
Clay Miner	2	3¾	2	5¼
Fitter's Assistant	2	3	2	4½
Boy Washing Stones	Yardage rate plus ½d.			

Appendix Five

Memorandum re Closure of GVR, 1960

BRITISH RAILWAYS (WESTERN REGION).

21st July, 1960.

MEMORANDUM,

KIDWELLY TO MYNYDD-Y-GARREG BRANCH.

The above single line freight branch, 2 miles 14 chains in length,was used to serve prIvate siding accommodation only but no traffic has passed since February 1959. Three firms had accommodation on the branch, all of whose private siding agreements have been terminated wIth their concurrence, the last as from May 1960.

In the circumstances, as the branch is no longer used by these or any other traders and there is no knowledge of any future developments which would justify the retention of the line, it is proposed to close it as from 29th August 1960 and the Committee are hereby informed of the position.

Divisional Traffic Manager,
45 Park Place,
CARDIFF.

Sources and Bibliography

Much of the primary source material relating to the Carmarthen & Cardigan Railway and the Gwendraeth Valleys Railway is held at the Public Record Office at Kew, under RAIL 99 and RAIL 285 respectively. There are also a few references to be found under RAIL 1057, whilst details of some of the industrial concerns associated with the railway are located under BT 31. The House of Lords Record Office kindly made available evidence taken before the passing of the 1865 and 1866 Acts, and additional information on the Parliamentary history of these and other railway proposals can be seen at the County Record Office, Carmarthen. The National Library of Wales, Aberystwyth, the Carmarthen Public Library and the Llanelli Public Library have excellent collections of local newspapers. For the purpose of this study, *The Carmarthen Journal* (founded 1810) and the *Llanelly Guardian* (1863-1953) in particular have been consulted.

In spite of its long independence from the BP&GVR, the Gwendraeth Valleys Railway has often been bracketed with it by writers. In 1977 S. Richards covered both lines in a privately published booklet, at the same period R.E. Bowen's article on the BP&GVR published in *The Carmarthenshire Antiquary* in 1976 was reprinted as a separate booklet. Other articles of note may be summarised as follows:

GWR Magazine vol. 35, 1923, p.61
Trains Illustrated vol. 5, 1952, p.370 and 418 - J. Bourne
Railway Magazine vol. 99, 1953, p.737 - J. Bourne
Steam Days, No. 58, June 1994, p.367 - M. Smith

Other helpful secondary sources must be noted, namely the *History of Kidwelly* by Revd D. Daven Jones, published at Carmarthen (1908) and *Saint Teilo's Church, Mynydd-y-Garreg* by Eric Hughes, published locally in 1992, and also *A Llanelli Chronicle* compiled by Gareth Hughes, published in 1986.

GWR No. 1378 *Margaret* in preservation at Scolton Manor Museum, Pembrokeshire, September 1981.   *Author*

Acknowledgements

Grateful thanks are due to all those mentioned here, and not least the immensely helpful staff of several libraries and archives:

The Public Record Office; The House of Lords Record Office; The National Library of Wales, Aberystwyth; The Welsh Industrial & Maritime Museum, Cardiff; The Dyfed County Record Office, Carmarthen; The Carmarthen Public Library; The Llanelli Public Library; The GWR Museum, Swindon, and Thamesdown Borough Council; The British Geological Survey, and The Industrial Railway Society.

R. ab Elis, Dr J. Alexander, E. Anthony, W. Baker, R.E. Bowen, T. Charlton, B. Cripps, T. David, A.G. Davies, F.K. Davies, J.D. Davies, V. Emmanuel, P.V. Evans, T.J. Evans, L. Francis, D.B. Gravell, Mrs I. Gravell, T. Gravell, T. Griffiths, V. Griffiths, M. Hale, J. de Havilland, E. Hughes, J. John, D. Jones, F. Jones, R.W. Kidner, A. Lewis, E.J. Miller, R.L. Pittard, R. Protheroe-Jones, P. Reynolds, R. Roberts, R. Simmonds, W. Thomas, J. Walters, R. Walters, R. Worsley.

Index